JOHN WAYNE

JOHN WAYNE

A Pyramid Illustrated History of the Movies

by
ALAN G. BARBOUR

General Editor: **TED SENNETT**

PYRAMID
PUBLICATIONS
NEW YORK

Pyramid Illustrated History of the Movies

Copyright © 1974 by Pyramid Communications, Inc.

First edition published July, 1974

ISBN 0-515-03481-9
Library of Congress Catalog Card Number: 74-1568

Printed in the United States of America

Pyramid Books are published by Pyramid Communications, Inc. Its trademarks, consisting of the word "Pyramid" and the portrayal of a pyramid, are registered in the United States Patent Office.

PYRAMID COMMUNICATIONS, INC.
919 Third Avenue, New York, N.Y. 10022

(graphic design by anthony basile)

Dedicated with love to my wife,
Catherine Jean Barbour

ACKNOWLEDGMENTS

I should like to thank the following people and organizations for their generous assistance in the preparation of this book: Allied Artists, Jean Barbour, Batjac Productions, Ernest Burns, Cinemabilia, John Cocchi, Columbia Pictures Corp., The Film and Theatre Collection at the Lincoln Center branch of the New York Public Library, Jack Klaw, Paula Klaw, Alvin H. Marill, Doug McClelland, The Memory Shop, MGM, Monogram Pictures, Movie Star News, Music Corporation of America, National General Pictures, National Telefilm Associates, Inc., Paramount Pictures Corp., Premium Products, Inc., Republic Pictures Corp., Mark Ricci, RKO Radio Pictures, Seven Arts, Inc., Steve Sallay, Twentieth Century-Fox, Inc., United Artists Corp., Universal Pictures Corp., Jerry Vermilye, Warner Brothers, Inc. (Arthur Wilson); and a very special thank you to my editor, Ted Sennett.

CONTENTS

THE IMAGE

Most film critics do not particularly care for John Wayne. They dislike his films, heap scorn on his performances, are appalled by his politics and, indeed, find no real interest even in the man himself. Fortunately, the critics are not very important to Wayne. They are not the ones who made him the star he has been for nearly one-half of his forty-seven-year career.

Then who *does* like John Wayne? His fans. There are millions of them and they, not the critics, are the ones who have spent over four hundred million of their hard-earned dollars to see John Wayne in action on the screen over the years. To these people, from presidents to the average man in the street, he is not only one of their favorite actors, but a symbol of rugged, virtuous heroism. They call him a "great American," and that's a tribute only one other performer has merited with equal consistency in the last thirty years: Bob Hope. However, Hope didn't win his accolades for his film work, but rather for his close association with American fighting men through three long, turbulent wars.

Why has John Wayne reached this lofty peak of adulation with filmgoers? Primarily for two basic reasons that are easily discernible: their identity with the type of characters he portrays on screen and their approval of his fundamental, unwavering philosophy about himself and his country offscreen. The first of these reasons is by far more important.

Before we examine Wayne's screen identity, we should state a simple statistic. Wayne has appeared on the screen since 1927. Forty-seven years! This means that the two-thirds of the American population who are approximately fifty-five years of age or younger has seen Wayne in films all of their moviegoing lives, and they have seem him most frequently playing a hero. As a result of this continual exposure, he has become a heroic figure to many of these people, and the screen's most consistent personification of what we have fantasized to be the legendary hero of the Old West.

Although the American Revolution was a significant period in our history, it has never been depicted adequately on the screen, nor has it really captured the imagination of filmgoers. Too complex in its conflicting events, too removed from the present in speech and dress, the late eighteenth century has not been a favorite era with filmmakers. There also seemed to be a lack of strong *individual* heroism in the

Revolutionary years. Everyone appeared to be working in unison, or at least in small groups, toward common goals.

The opening of the West a century later was an entirely different story. This time the stress was more on individual heroics: the pioneer wife in her struggle for survival, the Indian scout braving hostile territory, the marshal who brought the rule of law to a lawless land, and others equally courageous. And the drama of their lives seems to have been played amidst the grandeur of the most beautiful and spectacular scenery in the country. Small wonder that this period adapted itself so well to legend and myth on the movie screens, and it was the virtues we tend to associate with these hardy people that we see in the Western portrayals of John Wayne. Roy Paul Madsen in his book, *The Impact of Film*, has very neatly pinpointed the basic conventions we associate with our Western heroes: "The Westerner is the last 'man of honor' and his cinematic genre one of the few film forms in which the concept of personal integrity retains its credibility. His archaic code of conduct would make him appear ridiculous by contemporary standards if it were not for the fact that he is potentially willing to kill or be killed rather than to compromise his integrity. He is self-defined, self-contained, and demands that all others accept him on his own terms. He judges himself by a rigid standard of deportment—courage regardless of the odds."*

To this basic concept, Wayne, in his portrayals, has added the more simple human elements individuals can identify with readily: honesty, loyalty, compassion, and dedication. Very likely the single most important quality Wayne possessed was masculinity. Six-foot-four, handsome and ruggedly built, he has been the personification of the ideal American male. He was also an ethnic neuter, his appeal reaching all ages and groups of viewers.

The same ideals Wayne pictured in his Westerns were also visible in his war films. Once again courage was all-important, but new ingredients were added—honor, duty, self-sacrifice, unquestioning patriotism and the abilities requisite to be a leader of men. Men, who form the largest percentage of Wayne's fans, have been drawn to him by an almost inherent admiration for the actor's apparent raw courage in the face of disaster or death. Through his deeds, his adventures, they fulfill their escapist fantasies, and this is no doubt why he has built up such a loyal following.

Of secondary importance to

*Madsen, Roy Paul, *The Impact of Film*, Macmillan, New York, 1973, p. 266.

Wayne's image is his personal brand of patriotism, his unceasing praise for the more pleasant, more time-honored aspects of the American way of life. Some call him a "super-patriot," indignant that he tends to gloss over all the bad and stress the good, but he is hardly bothered by this. Without apology or regret, Wayne admits to being an old-fashioned, honest-to-goodness, flag-waving patriot. Perhaps it is his Midwestern heritage that helped to inspire this attitude, or maybe an acquired set of principles that form the basis for his belief. Whatever the reasons, when Wayne says, "I thank God every day of my life that I'm an American," few people can disbelieve his sincerity. By combining this real-life attitude with the fictional Western hero he has created on screen, one can see why he is very likely the most popular American screen actor of all time.

All this is not completely one-sided, however. Wayne's detractors, though decidedly in the minority, are a particularly vociferous lot. They see in Wayne's screenwork not a glorification of the great American hero, but the perpetuation of the great American myth. They resent his treatment of minorities, particularly Indians, in his Westerns and they detest the false heroics and glorification of blind courage in his war films. And they absolutely refuse to dis-associate Wayne's screen portrayals from his personal attitudes and views. Wayne can understand their viewpoint, but he has no special tolerance for many of these people when his brand of patriotism is challenged by them.

Time is becoming John Wayne's only real enemy. He is the last of his breed of screen animal; an en-dangered species, to be sure. All of his competition has vanished. Gary Cooper and Audie Murphy are dead. Randolph Scott and Joel McCrea are retired. Burt Lancaster, Kirk Douglas, Henry Fonda, Gregory Peck and James Stewart have left the West for urban settings where more urgent concerns can be met. When John Wayne finally de-parts who will be left to embody and perpetuate the myth? The answer is simple: Nobody!

Wayne's widest appeal and strongest support has always been found in that broad spectrum of the American populace somewhat ambiguously defined as Middle America. His recognizable screen image through the years has been fashioned primarily from the amalgamation of idealistic, pioneerlike virtues: honesty, integrity, loyalty, and a bedrock belief in dedicated hard work and the "rightness" of the American way. It is a well-deserved kinship, for the seeds of Wayne's existence were sown and reaped in the midst of this Utopian-like fortress of Americana.

Marion Michael Morrison was the name given to the first-born child of Clyde and Mary Morrison on May 26, 1907 in the small town of Winterset, Iowa. A younger brother, Bob, followed soon after. The Morrisons operated a small pharmacy with a stoically dedicated determination derived in no small part from their Scottish and Irish heritage. A combination of bad health, resulting from the harshness of severe, cold winters, and financial insolvency forced the family to seek a hopefully better life, and in 1913 they moved to a small ranch in Palmdale, California. Working in an area bordering the hot, barren wastes of the Mojave Desert, the family found themselves engaged in a test of endurance as they tended their crops of corn and peas. Young

THE MAN

Michael took the hardships all in stride, hewing out of them the strength and determination that turned the boy into the man.

He attended a school eight miles from home at Lancaster, riding there on the family horse and enjoying for the first time the exhilaration of riding an animal across the land. Unfortunately, the Morrisons' farming venture was a short-lived affair. After two years the family again found itself insolvent and another move was made, this time to Glendale where Clyde once again went into the drug business.

During these early years, Michael began his love affair with the movies. Throughout the week he worked in a number of odd jobs to contribute to the family's income, and one of those jobs was distributing handbills for the local theater. In return he was allowed to see all the movies free of charge. Fascinated by the flickering images on the screen, he became addicted to the larger-than-life celluloid heroes: Tom Mix, William S. Hart, Harry Carey, Hoot Gibson, Buck Jones, and daredevil action star, Douglas Fairbanks, Sr.

It was while in Glendale that Michael first acquired his nickname

As a young actor

"Duke." As the story is often told, he owned a large Airedale dog named "Duke." When he went to school he would leave the animal in the care of some friendly firemen at the local firehouse. The men nicknamed the dog's master "Little Duke" and the "Little" was dropped as Michael grew tall. "Duke" persisted over the years.

At high school in Glendale, Michael worked diligently and became an honor student as well as the president of his senior class. His extracurricular activities included debating and football. After graduation it was Michael's ambition to go to the United States Naval Academy at Annapolis, but that dream was shattered when he placed only fourth on the list of eligibles. As an alternative he elected to attend the University of Southern California on a football scholarship in 1925. The scholarship scarcely covered his expenses and he found himself once again doing odd jobs to make ends meet. In the meantime, his father left the drugstore and set up his own ice-cream company, another ill-fated effort which lasted only long enough to see him return a third time to pharmacy.

Michael's first contact with moviemaking came during his tenure at USC. Constantly searching for new sources of income, he asked his football coach, Howard Jones, for some leads. Jones, who knew many of the leading figures of the film industry—they sought him out for tickets to important games —talked Tom Mix into obtaining summer jobs for Michael and his close friend, Don Williams, at Fox Studios, where Mix was a top star. At the studio, Mix turned the young men over to director George Marshall who started them out as set-dressers and prop men at a salary of thirty-five dollars a week —big money for Michael in those days. Caught up in the special aura that surrounds moviemaking, Michael soon fell under the scrutiny of director John Ford who used him first only as a prop man and then as a bit player. (Although most filmographies list his first screen appearances in 1928 Fox releases, he did make a brief onscreen appearance, plainly visible, though fleetingly, in the 1927 Richard Barthelmess First National release, *The Drop Kick*. He was one of ten college football stars who were chosen to appear in the film.)

John Ford, a severe taskmaster, frequently gave Michael a rough time, but soon grew to admire and respect the youngster who gave as much as he got. They were of the same breed—tough, honest, strong-minded men whose friendship endured throughout the director's lifetime. Other friendships sprouted in those days as well. Men like Ward Bond, Victor

As a young actor

McLaglen, Bruce Cabot, George O'Brien and Wayne film regulars Paul Fix and Grant Withers, fashioned themselves into a bawdy, boozing, brawling fraternity of dedicated performers.

Much as Ford admired the inexperienced youth, he could only give him small roles in his silent and early talkies. But the special quality Ford neglected to develop was noticed by fellow director Raoul Walsh. Walsh saw Michael lugging props about and was instantly struck by the young actor's demeanor. Checking with Ford, and receiving a strongly encouraging recommendation, Walsh put Michael, virtually unknown, into the leading role (originally intended for Gary Cooper) in his elaborate Western action spectacle, *The Big Trail* (1930). Though Michael was given the kind of a showcase most actors can only dream of receiving, it did not launch him on his career. The studio moguls at Fox, traditionally dense about developing raw talent, followed up this spectacle by casting Michael in a series of banal and ineffectual vehicles. The one definite change that did occur with *The Big Trail* was his name. Winfield Sheehan, the head of production at Fox, could not abide the name "Marion Morrison." He suggested "John Wayne" as much more suitable for his lanky, rugged new star.

Wayne's failure to catch on as a popular player was both disillusioning and disheartening for him. For the next ten years he sweated out his frustrations in the B-film factories of many studios, desperately trying to recapture the elusive stardom he felt he had been cheated out of. It wasn't all a waste; in those years he would learn more about the fundamentals and skills of moviemaking than most actors could acquire in their entire careers.

In 1933, still in the throes of poverty-row stardom, Wayne married his first wife, Josephine Saenz, the darkhaired daughter of the Panamanian consul in Los Angeles. Within the year the Waynes had their first child, son Michael. In rapid succession came daughter Toni, second son Patrick, and second daughter Melinda. To support his expanding family, Wayne drove himself slavishly during those hectic days of the thirties. Driven by ambition, working the long hours of the studio mills in those years, he spent too little time at home. His marriage was headed for failure.

Wayne cast off his B-film image when his old friend, John Ford, selected him for a primary role in his trend-setting Western film, *Stagecoach*, in 1939. After completing his contractual obligation to Republic to star in a series of low-budget but extremely popular Three Mesquiteer Westerns, he

THE BIG TRAIL (1930). His first starring role

was never again to appear in anything less than major productions. But bigger productions meant even more time away from his wife and children. Josephine, who never approved of her husband's choice of rowdy friends and his continued absence from home, finally reached the end of her patience. The final break came in 1942 when the couple separated.

With a family and over thirty, Wayne was not accepted for service during World War II, even though he tried to enlist. He did, however, make numerous tours to visit overseas hospitals and the men in the war zones were grateful just to see and listen to the star who offered encouragement and brought a welcome taste of home to them.

After the war Wayne, now the most popular action star in films, went to Mexico on a routine business venture, where he met Esperanza Bauer, a diplomat's daughter who was being signed to a contract by Republic. (She never succeeded as an actress.) In January 1946 she became the second Mrs.

Wayne. Wayne's good friend Ward Bond was the best man. It was a stormy union with frequent battles erupting between the volatile couple. There were no children this time, and the pair split acrimoniously in 1953 shortly after Wayne had completed *The Quiet Man*. Wayne was incensed that his wife chose to unveil many private family matters in public.

Alone again, Wayne plunged into his work, but his films in the fifties were a highly mixed lot, both good and bad, with a disturbing leaning toward the latter. Awaiting his separation from Esperanza,

he went to Peru to scout possible locations for what he hoped would be his biggest film production, *The Alamo*. There he met and was attracted to Pilar Palette, a beautiful Peruvian film star. They met again in Hollywood where Pilar had come to do some postproduction work on one of her films. When Wayne went to Hawaii to do scenes for *The Sea Chase* he invited Pilar to come along. When his divorce became final, they were married on November 1, 1954.

Pilar and Wayne seemed to be well matched in temperament and points of view. Three more children

THE BIG TRAIL (1930). With Ian Keith and Marguerite Churchill

STAGECOACH (1939). As The Ringo Kid

Second wife Esperanza

became members of the growing Wayne dynasty: Aissa, Ethan (named for the character Wayne played in *The Searchers*) and Marisa. Wayne appeared to play the real-life role of father far more successfully than many of his screen roles, offering more compassion and tolerance than his rock-hard screen image could ever reveal. For nearly twenty years his pride in his family rose with the actor's pride in his work.

For one brief period, however, all that he had built almost disappeared overnight as the one project he had dreamed of completing nearly plummeted him into finan-

Third wife Pilar

cial ruin. *The Alamo* was an elaborate and expensive film and needed
large financial backing. Wayne put
all of his own money into the project
and when the 1960 spectacle failed
to return the grosses he expected,
he found himself facing complete
insolvency. It took a great deal of
determined effort and five years of
back-breaking work before he

THE ALAMO (1960). As Davy Crockett

THE COWBOYS (1972). As Will Anderson

began working his way once again to financial stability. Just when the future appeared more secure, a more personal tragedy threatened. During a routine examination in September of 1964, doctors found cancer pinpointed in the actor's lungs. Wayne entered Good Samaritan Hospital in Los Angeles for an operation. Happily it was a success, and Wayne set about re-evaluating his goals in life.

The past ten years have been generally happy and productive for Wayne. He won a well-deserved Academy Award for *True Grit* and his film work continues to improve in quality and scope. Yet, for all that, there have been personal troubles. After nineteen years of marriage, Pilar and Wayne announced they were separating. The actor, who has always tried to keep his family problems away from the public, refuses to discuss the reasons for the breakup.

Wayne's popularity continues unabated through the seventies. His films over the years have grossed more than four hundred million dollars, a record unmatched by any other star in history. For more than twenty years he has been on the list of box-office favorites around the world. In 1969 he was voted the "Superstar of the Decade" and the longest-reigning top star in film history. Hardly a week goes by that several of his films are not featured on the nation's television sets, usually playing to top ratings.

There is no mysterious reason for his success. He inspires no avant-garde adulation, generates no special mystique. Nor does he cater to film buffs who find continued comfort in the warm womb of nostalgia. It is as simple as this: he gives the people what they *want* to see, and, what is more important to his producers, what the people are willing, if not downright anxious to *pay* to see. Not a bad position for a sixty-seven-year-old father of seven and a grandfather of twenty.

The sum total of John Wayne's screen work to date is so substantial that it is a difficult task to select a mere ten titles and say with any degree of certainty that these choices represent his best films. Although there are five titles that virtually everyone will agree are superior Wayne vehicles (*Stagecoach*, *Red River*, *She Wore a Yellow Ribbon*, *The Quiet Man*, and *True Grit*), the remaining five films are open to dispute and a matter of personal judgment. For every vote cast in favor of *The Searchers*, you could probably find a similarly strong voice raised in favor of *Hondo*, and *The Man Who Shot Liberty Valance* might be easily offset by a preference for *Three Godfathers*. The weakest entry is clearly *The Alamo*. Though its spectacularly staged battle sequences are among the best ever filmed, the plot construction is extremely shaky and the characterizations are cardboard; yet it belongs on the list because it was Wayne's most personal contribution to his film career.

General characteristics are easily discernible in all these films. With the exception of *The Alamo*, which Wayne directed himself, all the remaining titles were helmed by tough, hard-nosed men (Ford, Hathaway, Hawks, Dwan) who had developed film expertise over many years and were able to channel Wayne's massive screen personality

THE ESSENTIAL WAYNE

Stagecoach (1939)
Red River (1948)
She Wore A Yellow Ribbon (1949)
Sands Of Iwo Jima (1949)
The Quiet Man (1952)
The Searchers (1956)
Rio Bravo (1959)
The Alamo (1960)
The Man Who Shot Liberty Valance (1962)
True Grit (1969)

into more restrained and creative boundaries. Again excluding *The Alamo*, all of these films had strong and believable scripts and in every case the photography was exemplary. One would think that this combination of superb direction, writing and photography would be easy to come by in a Hollywood of seasoned professionals but, as shown by the small percentage of outstanding Wayne films over a forty-seven year span of time, such was not the case.

Until the 1939 production of *Stagecoach*, John Ford had not made a Western film since his silent *Three Bad Men* in 1926, and he entered into the project with vast enthusiasm. For the first time he

STAGECOACH (1939). With Claire Trevor

planned to make extensive use of the spectacular natural features of Monument Valley (which later came to be known affectionately as "Ford Country") to shoot many of the exterior action sequences. In addition he had lined up an impressive cast headed by Claire Trevor, Thomas Mitchell, John Carradine, George Bancroft and Andy Devine. The only role he had not yet filled was the pivotal one of the Ringo Kid. Several years earlier, he had shown a copy of the screenplay to Wayne, asking him if he could recommend anyone who could handle the role. Wayne, who had often thought Ford was purposely avoiding him during those dog days of the early thirties when he was working feverishly to achieve recognition, was in the midst of shooting a series of B-Westerns for Republic. Out of courtesy he read the script and made what he felt were several good recommendations (Lloyd Nolan was one of his choices.)

Suddenly, to his surprise, Ford shouted, "How about you, Duke? Can't you handle it?" Wayne, incredulous but game, quickly told the director that he could handle the job. Ford took the young actor at his word and for three years, while Wayne kept hoping he would get the coveted role, Ford continued to pressure the studio officials, who were opposed to using an actor regarded as a poverty-row saddle ace, into letting the "kid" play Ringo. Ford was adamant and eventually won his battle. Wayne received permission from his bosses at Republic and started working on *Stagecoach*, the film that would finally launch him on his rise to screen stardom.

By today's more critical standards, the Dudley Nichols screenplay (based on *Stage to Lordsburg* by Ernest Haycox) is actually rather pedestrian and cliché-ridden—a kind of glorified soap opera with an occasional burst of action to keep the audiences awake and interested. Six disparate travelers: a booze-soaked doctor (Mitchell), a gambler (Carradine), a whiskey drummer (Donald Meek), a pregnant wife (Louise Platt), a cafe dancer (Claire Trevor) run out of town by indignant womenfolk, and a banker turned embezzler (Berton Churchill), are going to Lordsburg on a stage driven by Bucky (Andy Devine) and a U.S. marshal (George Bancroft). On their route they pick up the Ringo Kid (Wayne) whose horse has become lame. The Kid is on his way to a showdown with the notorious Plummer brothers (Tom Tyler, Joe Rickson, Vester Pegg). Giving himself up to the marshal, Ringo joins the other passengers. The stage arrives at an overnight rest stop and, in rapid-fire succession, Ringo falls for Dallas (Trevor), Lucy Mallory (Platt) has her baby with the aid of a sobered-up Doc Boone

STAGECOACH (1939). With Andy Devine and George Bancroft

STAGECOACH (1939). With George Bancroft and Louise Platt

(Mitchell) and the whole group learns that the Indians are on the warpath. The next morning the stage heads out and the Indians attack (in a now-classic chase across the salt flats which has often been copied but never equaled for creative spectacle). The cavalry, bugles blowing, arrives in time to ward off the attackers but Peacock (Meek) is wounded and Hatfield (Carradine) killed. The stage finally arrives at Lordsburg and the marshal allows Ringo to engage in his determined showdown. The Kid guns down his enemies and is himself wounded. Curley (Bancroft) goes soft and sends Ringo and Dal-las across the border to safety and the start of a new life.

This is hardly an original plot line, and even in 1939 there was little new in *Stagecoach* that had not been used many times before. What *was* new was the scope and inventiveness of Ford's direction, the remarkable crispness of his cinematic imagery. Each of the characterizations was so artfully written by Nichols that it seemed newly minted rather than stale, and the action scenes were magnificently staged and photographed. Leading stuntman Yakima Canutt helped plan many of the sequences, and Bert Glennon's camera beautifully caught the sweep and the starkness of the Western landscape. The distinctive music score was fashioned from numerous early folk songs and won an Academy Award for Richard Hageman and his collaborators, W. Franke Harling, John Leipold, and Leo Shuken. A second Academy Award went to Thomas Mitchell as Best Supporting Actor for his performance as the bibulous doctor.

Ford did not give Wayne an easy time during the filming. He berated, cajoled, tormented, tricked and otherwise abused the insecure actor into giving the best performance of his career to that date. At the time Ford may have seemed insensitive to the feelings of the younger man, but the director realized that he would have to be brutal to raise the level of Wayne's performance to that of the other players. He was determined to keep Wayne from doing a weak and ineffectual job in contrast to the polished acting of the professionals surrounding him. It worked, and one need only view Wayne's performances in films released the same year to see the remarkable difference.

Stagecoach not only launched Wayne's new career, it also reawakened Hollywood's interest in the genre, and a series of major Westerns followed. In 1966, *Stagecoach* was remade with a cast headed by Bing Crosby (in Mitchell's role), Alex Cord (as Ringo), and Ann-Margret (as Dallas). It was a failure, and only served to reinforce the classic qualities of Ford's original.

For the nine years following *Stagecoach*, Wayne appeared in a variety of roles that satisfied the public's appetite for action but few of them demanded much in the way of acting acumen. Skillfully but routinely, he walked through most of them, tending to support the fact that one of the most important but least appreciated aspects of filmmaking is a good script. Wayne finally found a solid story and a strong director in Howard Hawks' 1948 production of *Red River*. Based on Borden Chase's *Saturday Evening Post* story, "The Chisholm Trail," the screenplay by Chase and Charles Schnee was basically a camouflaged tale of the founding of the famous King Ranch empire that was built up in early Texas. *Red River* centered on Thomas Dunson (Wayne) and his foster son Garth (Montgomery Clift), who build a vast cattle empire after the end of the Civil War. To market their beef, they head a massive cattle drive over the Chisholm Trail, past the Red River and into Kansas City. Dunson is a virtual tyrant throughout the long, grueling trek, frequently taking the law into his own hands to handle transgressors. Eventually he earns the

RED RIVER (1948). With Montgomery Clift

enmity of Garth, who wrests control of the herd from Dunson and heads on his own to sell the cattle for both of them. Dunson threatens to kill the boy and tracks him down relentlessly to the railhead where, in a well-remembered confrontation scene, they battle viciously. Garth's girlfriend Tess (Joanne Dru) succeeds in breaking up the fight and the two men are reconciled.

Red River was filmed in grandiose style by Hawks, whose knowledge of and feeling for the Western terrain matched John Ford's. Fre-

quently, the screen was filled with strikingly effective images of massive cattle herds moving in panoramic display. The resilience and camaraderie of rough-hewn men under stress (a favorite theme of Hawks') was conveyed by a well-chosen cast. The film was also aided by an appropriately driving and forceful score by Dimitri Tiomkin and by the stark, exquisitely crafted black-and-white photography of Russell Harlan. Hawks, who likes to augment his work with comedy whenever the occasion permits, offset the violence in the film by unleashing Walter Brennan in his most characteristic style as an earthy, toothless varmint.

Hawks, like Ford, was a forceful director who worked himself and his actors hard to achieve a high degree of professionalism. Wayne was concerned that he and Clift might not be able to generate any real excitement together, particularly in the fight sequence where the six-foot-four Wayne towered over his more diminutive co-star. Wayne was also wary of "method" actors whose motivational "mumbo-jumbo" tends to turn nonmethod performers sour. Hawks convinced Wayne that the newcomer could more than handle his end of the assignment. As it turned out, Clift's performance was equal to, if not in some ways better than, Wayne's own solid characterization. The critics generally liked the film and Bosley Crowther seemed to state the majority opinion in *The New York Times* when he wrote that the many excellent performances were "topped off by a withering job of acting a boss-wrangler done by Mr. Wayne. This consistently able portrayer of two-fisted, two-gunned outdoor men surpasses himself in this picture."

Red River, however, has not received unanimous acclaim. Although many critics consider it to be

RED RIVER (1948). With Walter Brennan

RED RIVER (1948). With Montgomery Clift

the best Western film of the forties, there are those who feel it is little more than a restatement of earlier Western film themes. Others find a certain harshness in Hawks' handling of the subject as contrasted with the more humanized treatment of the Western milieu by Ford. It is a somewhat prejudicial evaluation, to be sure, made largely by extremely partisan Ford fans. Yet *Red River* remains a highly regarded Western drama which seems to gain added stature over the years, especially when one remembers that it was Hawks' first attempt at handling the genre. As

was the case with *Stagecoach* almost a decade earlier, *Red River* reawakened a floundering interest in the Western.

Just before Wayne's appearance in *Red River*, Ford had directed him in the first of his famous "cavalry trilogy" films, *Fort Apache*. It was a good film, with vigorous action scenes and well-honed character portraits, but it was really Henry Fonda who had the stronger role and more his film than Wayne's. However, in *She Wore a Yellow Ribbon* (1949), the second film in the trilogy, Wayne had the dominant role. The film turned out to be a superb vehicle for the actor and gave him one of his favorite screen roles. Bosley Crowther again singled the actor's work out for praise in his *New York Times* review of the film: "Mr. Wayne, his hair streaked with silver and wearing a dashing mustache, is the absolute image and ideal of the legendary cavalryman."

The screenplay for *She Wore a Yellow Ribbon* by Frank S. Nugent and Laurence Stallings was based on a *Saturday Evening Post* story by James Warner Bellah (who later co-authored the screenplay for *The Man Who Shot Liberty Valance*). In the well-enacted story, Captain Brittles (Wayne) is asked to take one last assignment before retirement. The Indians have begun a new war and he must intercept them and, at the same time, escort the major's wife (Mildred Natwick) and her daughter, Olivia (Joanne Dru), to safety. When they arrive at their destination (a stage depot), they find it destroyed and the residents massacred. The troop returns with the women to the fort. The Indians, in the interval, acquire a supply of guns and ammunition and threaten to unleash devastation on the cavalrymen. Brittles, back at the fort, is relieved of his command because of his impending retirement and Lt. Pennell (Harry Carey, Jr.) leads the troop into battle. Brittles, concerned over the inexperience of the younger man, rides out and initiates a plan of his own. In the climax, his soldiers stampede the Indians' horses and the Indians are forced to retreat. Brittles returns to the fort and learns that he has been appointed Chief of Civilian Scouts, thus allowing him to stay with the outfit he had loved commanding for so long.

In a rare switch for the genre, the action sequences of *She Wore a Yellow Ribbon* seemed almost of secondary importance to the full-blooded character studies. As usual, the director enjoyed making expansive use of the comic abilities of his players (particularly Victor McLaglen), and the cast indulged themselves fully. McLaglen, Harry Carey, Jr., Ben Johnson, Mildred Natwick, Arthur Shields and especially Wayne came through with warmly human vignettes. The film was a virtual mother lode of sentimentality, particularly evident in the scenes in which Wayne places flowers on his wife's grave and then, in a solemn soliloquy, proceeds to bring her up-to-date on current events. In less capable hands than Wayne's or Ford's, these sequences might well have become farcical.

Of enormous value to the film's overall effectiveness was the glowing color photography which won cameraman Winton Hoch an Academy Award and brought out the splendor of Monument Valley

SHE WORE A YELLOW RIBBON (1949). As Captain Brittles

perhaps more than in any other Western film. Ford was especially pleased with the results he achieved with this film. In Peter Bogdanovich's treatise, *John Ford*, the director said, "I tried to copy the Remington style there—you can't copy him one hundred percent—but at least I tried to get in his color and movement, and I think I succeeded partly."*

Wayne's attempts to play believable war heroes in the forties were generally ineffectual, hampered by

*Peter Bogdanovich, *John Ford:* University of California Press, Berkeley, Calif. 1968, p. 87

poor scripts and his highly simplistic, one-dimensional approach to the subject. The films were effective wartime propaganda, but their heroics were purely fabricated. Unfortunately, war *is* hell, and the men who fight are not all so willing to give up their lives recklessly. Yet, at the end of the decade, Wayne succeeded with one war film: *Sands of Iwo Jima* (1949). Written by Harry Brown and Wayne's good friend James Edward Grant (and based on a story by Brown), the film starred Wayne in a solid role built around a more believable war situation. As

SHE WORE A YELLOW RIBBON (1949). With Victor McLaglen

SHE WORE A YELLOW RIBBON (1949). With Ben Johnson

Sergeant John M. Stryker, Wayne ruthlessly converts his assigned novices into trained killers. They naturally grow to hate the tyranny of the tough leader, but after several brutal encounters with the enemy they acquire a deep respect for the man. Amidst the action the film interweaves a series of personal stories. The film reaches a tragic, but predictable, conclusion when Stryker is shot and killed by a sniper while he is routinely lighting a cigarette, confident that the worst of the battle is over.

The highlights of *Sands of Iwo Jima* were the exceptionally well-staged battle sequences with outstanding pyrotechnics supplied under the special effects aegis of Republic's top craftsmen, Howard and Theodore Lydecker. The film's director, Allan Dwan, was also able to skillfully intercut actual newsreel footage into the staged sequences to add a greater feeling of authenticity. This footage included the famous flag raising on Mt. Suribachi which was recreated in closeup and matched almost perfectly the newsreel record of the actual incident.

Wayne was the very picture of determination and forcefulness in his role as Stryker. The *New York Times* critic noted that "Wayne is especially honest and convincing, for he manages to dominate a screenplay which is crowded with exciting, sweeping battle scenes. His performance holds the picture together." His fellow actors evidently were similarly impressed as well for they nominated Wayne for an Academy Award, his first such recognition. Unfortunately he lost out to his friend Broderick Crawford's memorable performance in *All the King's Men*.

In 1950 Wayne completed Ford's cavalry film cycle by starring in *Rio Grande*. It was the weakest of the three films, but it was picturesque and had many typical Ford features. Two years later star and director teamed up again for Ford's colorful, idyllic excursion to the land of his ancestors, Innisfree, Ireland. Ford always liked to refer to his 1952 production of *The Quiet Man* as his first real love story. Once again the master brewed his stylized mixture of raucous comedy, sentimentality and virile action to fashion another classic film. Of course he had a lot of help from his friends. Turning such Hibernian veterans as Victor McLaglen, Barry Fitzgerald, Arthur Shields, Ward Bond, and Wayne loose on the Ould Sod was like engaging in a holiday with pay for the crusty director, and everything seemed to work ideally.

The screenplay by Frank S. Nugent, based on a story by Maurice Walsh, was carefully crafted to accentuate every possi-

SANDS OF IWO JIMA (1949). With Forrest Tucker

SANDS OF IWO JIMA (1949). With John Agar

ble comic opportunity. The straightforward plot found Sean Thornton (Wayne), an American prizefighter who had given up the sport after killing an opponent, returning home to Ireland. His purchase of a piece of property earns the enmity of Danaher (McLaglen) who wants the real estate himself. To complicate matters, Sean falls in love with Danaher's sister, Mary Kate (Maureen O'Hara), and eventually marries her. In a dispute over Mary Kate's dowry, Danaher tries to get Sean to fight him, but Sean, remembering the death he had caused earlier, refuses to fight. Mary Kate accuses her husband of cowardice and leaves him, but Sean follows, pulls her off a train and literally drags her home. Danaher and Sean finally meet and engage in a donnybrook that ranges all over the colorful landscape. Sean wins and the couple are hap-

THE QUIET MAN (1952). With Barry Fitzgerald

pily reunited.

Combining pastoral beauty with the sort of rowdy Irish comedy Ford always favored in his films, *The Quiet Man* delighted movie audiences. The performances were all superb, highlighted by Barry Fitzgerald's hilarious and endearing portrait of the incorrigible Michaeleen Flynn ("A fine soft morning," he remarks, his eyes fairly twinkling with the trouble he anticipates.)

All the elements of the film were in as perfect harmony as the Irish landscape. Victor Young composed an entertaining blend of familiar Irish melodies and original themes, and it was among the first film scores to be issued on records. Another important ingredient in the success of the film was the breathtaking color photography which forever captured on film the exhilarating beauty of the countryside. Photographer Winton

Hoch added another Academy Award to the one he received for *She Wore a Yellow Ribbon*. Ford, who often touted *The Quiet Man* as one of his favorite films, was similarly honored when the Academy gave him its "Oscar" as Best Director of the Year. It was his sixth such honor. Wayne demonstrated that he was able to handle a delicately shaded and complex role with consummate skill and understanding.

Another strong performance was given by Wayne in the 1956 production of John Ford's *The Searchers*. Ford's earlier Westerns were a successful blend of action, comedy and a sort of pervasive if unreal optimism. With *The Searchers*, his enthusiasm for the genre became somewhat tinged with bitterness. The viewer is struck by the undercurrent of hopelessness and despair, of sorrow for sins past (particularly in his earlier treatment of the Indian), and an almost apologetic groping for forgiveness. Because of this rather sharp departure from previous conventions, *The Searchers* at times seems overly complex and confusing. The question is raised: to whom are we supposed to

THE QUIET MAN (1952). With Victor McLaglen

THE QUIET MAN (1952). With Maureen O'Hara

give our sympathy and support —the Indians or the vengeful whites?

The screenplay by Frank S. Nugent (a favorite writer of Ford's) was based on a novel by Alan LeMay. It focused on Ethan Edwards (Wayne), returning home several years after the end of the Civil War. Joining a posse in search of rustlers, he returns to find his family massacred and his two young daughters carried off by a brutal Indian, Chief Scar (Henry Brandon). Ethan sets out in pursuit and finds one of the girls dead. The search continues re-

lentlessly for five long years with setbacks due only to bad weather. In this passage of time his surviving daughter, Debbie (Natalie Wood), has grown up to young womanhood as an Indian. Ethan tries to rescue her, but is wounded by Chief Scar and is forced to return home. Later he learns that a troop of cavalry is about to attack the Indians and he joins them, intending to kill his daughter whom he feels has disgraced the family. When the ultimate confrontation is made, Ethan relents and takes his daughter home to begin a new life.

THE SEARCHERS (1956). As Ethan Edwards

THE SEARCHERS (1956). With Ward Bond

As usual, Ford staged many of his exteriors in Monument Valley, again using Winton Hoch to supply splendid color photography. The pictorial composition of many scenes in *The Searchers* are among the best to be found in any of Ford's Westerns, most notably in the moving final sequence in which Wayne reclaims his daughter.

The Searchers was produced by a newly formed but short-lived organization headed by Cornelius Vanderbilt Whitney, founder of New York's Whitney Museum, and in its advertising for the film proudly proclaimed the following: "We may not always succeed in our aims, but I promise that no C.V. Whitney picture will ever misrepresent or paint a false picture of the United States or its people." Somehow, one feels that the Indians found cold comfort in his statement.

Howard Hawks, having succeeded so admirably with *Red River*, began to appreciate the possibilities inherent in the genre. He also liked working with Wayne, and 1959's production of *Rio Bravo* proved to be a successful rematching of the pair. *Rio Bravo* was in complete contrast to Hawks' earlier work. *Red River* was expansive, a visual panorama almost epic in scope. In *Rio Bravo* Hawks seemed to reduce the genre to its very barest essentials. He concentrated on setting a few determined and heroic figures against the villains in the cramped environs of a few small interior sets. It is a long film that spends most of its time exploring the behavior patterns of its protagonists as they meet each new challenge. Jules Furthman and Leigh Brackett wrote the original screenplay that found Sheriff John T. Chance (Wayne) arresting Joe Burdette (Claude Akins) for murder. Joe's brother Nathan (John Russell) and his men surround the town to prevent Chance from taking his prisoner to the U.S. marshal. Chance's help comes in the form of a crippled deputy (Walter Brennan), an ex-deputy (Dean Martin) who is trying to fight off a bout of alcoholism, and a young gunfighter (Ricky Nelson). When Dude (Martin) is captured, a deal is set up to trade him for the prisoner. Through a ruse Dude is released and the prisoner is recaptured. Nathan and his cutthroats are captured or killed when the building they are hiding in is blown up with dynamite.

Hawks, who had vast experience in directing comedy (*20th Century*, *Bringing Up Baby*), once again utilized, as he had in *Red River*, Walter Brennan's highly personal brand of rawboned, crackling humor to provide a counterpoint to the drama and violence. Wayne's role was not of such depth that it merited any exceptional effort on his part. It did, however, create the

RIO BRAVO (1959). With Ricky Nelson

RIO BRAVO (1959). With Walter Brennan

model which Wayne was to use in many of his later films, a comfortable characterization that satisfied the requirements of his most accepted screen image.

Many consider *Rio Bravo* to be Hawks' best Western: a simplistic masterpiece. Two of the director's later films, *El Dorado* (1967) and *Rio Lobo* (1970) (both starring Wayne and with screenplays by Leigh Brackett who had coscripted *Rio Bravo*) had very similar plots, but were decidedly inferior and much less effective.

The Alamo (1960), though by no means giving Wayne his best role as an actor, must surely be considered his personal magnum opus—his most ambitious project ever. He had always believed that the true story of a small band of determined men, led by three great folk heroes (Davy Crockett, Jim Bowie and William Travis), willing to lay down their lives during Texas' epic struggle for independence, was one of the most heroic moments in American history. He felt the story had particular relevance in the fifties to a generation of young men who seemed not to understand or particularly care about what other generations had suffered to protect

52

the liberties they now so easily took for granted. He wanted to give them a history lesson cloaked in terms of spectacular entertainment.

Wayne had wanted to produce *The Alamo* as early as 1949 when he was still under contract to Republic, and he had even scouted locations in Panama. Herbert J. Yates, head of Republic Pictures, had encouraged Wayne in the project and then suddenly backed down. Annoyed at Yates' cavalier attitude towards a project he felt deeply about, the actor left the studio and made a new picture deal with Warner Bros. Ten years after his original plans had gone awry, Wayne received backing from United Artists. He spent $12,000,000 and three months of shooting time in Bracketville, Texas to make his historical tribute. Because of rising production costs he was forced to mortgage his company, Batjac, to raise almost $1,250,000 of his own money which he put into the project.

The completed film, which ran for a staggering three hours and nineteen minutes, was written by James Edward Grant, who had been constantly reworking the

THE ALAMO (1960). With Richard Widmark and Laurence Harvey

THE ALAMO (1960). As Davy Crockett

manuscript with Wayne for many years before production. Most of the film's running time was spent recounting the historical events leading up to the famous battle and the personal, though somewhat fictional, conflicts of the major participants: Sam Houston (Richard Boone), Crockett (Wayne), Bowie (Richard Widmark) and Travis (Laurence Harvey). The remaining footage featured some of the most spectacularly staged battle sequences ever created for an American film. Composer Dimitri Tiomkin provided an energetic and often lyrical background score. *The Alamo* received a total of eleven Academy Award nominations but only received one award, for sound.

Reviewers were not all kind to the film, many finding it tedious going but others hailed it as exciting screen entertainment. Wayne, who had both produced and directed *The Alamo* (his first effort behind the camera) could at least be assured that he had fulfilled his longtime dream in a most credible fashion.

Unfortunately, *The Alamo* did not make the money at the box office that he had hoped for and Wayne was almost wiped out financially. He eventually sold his percentage in the film to United Artists, and the company managed to recoup costs and make a profit on subsequent re-releases while Wayne barely broke even. Though he may not have made money on the film, he received an accolade that perhaps meant more to him. His old friend and mentor, John Ford, called *The Alamo* "the greatest picture I've ever seen."

Ford's more somber attitude toward the Western, which began with *The Searchers*, was even more pronounced in *The Man Who Shot Liberty Valance* (1962). A feeling of melancholia sweeps over us as we appear to be watching the last dying gasps of the mythic old West we had seen portrayed so often on the screen. It was like a final blow to the good-guys-versus-bad-guys heroics of the genre, and the beginning of a more clear-eyed, less romantic approach.

The highly original screenplay by James Warner Bellah and Willis Goldbeck opens with Senator Rance Stoddard (James Stewart) and his wife (Vera Miles) returning to a small town to attend the funeral of Tom Doniphon (Wayne), an old friend. Once there we are taken back through flashbacks to the days when Stoddard first arrived in town and was beaten up and robbed by a swaggering bully and killer, Liberty

THE ALAMO (1960). With Richard Widmark

THE MAN WHO SHOT LIBERTY VALANCE (1962). As Tom Doniphon

Valance (Lee Marvin). Doniphon brings Stoddard to a cafe where Hallie (Miles), the girl he loves, works as a waitress. Conflict grows when Hallie falls in love with Stoddard (inspiring a moving scene in which Doniphon burns down the addition to his ranch he had been building for her when he finds he has been spurned), and Valance challenges Stoddard to a gunfight. In a showdown the completely inexperienced Stoddard apparently guns down Valance and gains the reputation of "The Man Who Shot Liberty Valance." The title helps him win election to Congress. When Stoddard decides he doesn't want to be elected on a reputation for killing, Doniphon confesses that it was actually he who did the shooting. Stoddard gives in to Doniphon's pleas to continue his work and become a force for good. The flashbacks end and a reporter who has been taking notes tears them up. When asked why, he delivers the line which has almost become Wayne's real-life motto: "When the legend becomes a fact, print the legend!"

Wayne gave an exceptionally strong and convincing portrayal, though his role was considerably smaller than that of Stewart. An interesting touch was added to the film when Ford reused composer Alfred Newman's "Ann Rutledge" theme from his earlier film, *Young Mr. Lincoln* (1939) as background music. Often maintaining that film music was obtrusive, he nevertheless maintained great affection for this particular piece.

It has been claimed that author Charles Portis, with his eye on a future movie sale, fashioned the character of Rooster Cogburn in his best-selling novel *True Grit* specifically with Wayne in mind. Whether or not that is mere publicity is irrelevant. What does matter is that the 1969 film version gave Wayne a role he had been waiting to play for almost forty years. From the moment the actor read an advance set of galley proofs, he knew he had to play Rooster on screen. Trying to buy the rights for Batjac, he was outbid by producer Hal Wallis, but gladly settled to play the coveted role. It was very likely the smartest move Wayne had made in his long career. As Rooster, Wayne gave a bravura performance unlike anything he had ever done before. Wayne was to say that it was perfect type-casting, that Rooster was a "mean old bastard, a one-eyed, whiskey-soaked, sloppy old son-of-a-bitch—just like me!"

The screenplay by Marguerite Roberts remained fairly close to the novel (with the exception of a happier ending in which Mattie's arm was not amputated). In the story young Mattie Ross' (Kim Darby) father is killed by his hired hand,

THE MAN WHO SHOT LIBERTY VALANCE (1962). As Tom Doniphon

TRUE GRIT (1969). As Rooster Cogburn

Tom Chaney (Jeff Corey). Mattie, after completing arrangements for her father's funeral, seeks out a man with "true grit" to go after Chaney and bring him back. She finds this man in the person of Rooster Cogburn, a battered and irascible one-eyed U.S. marshal. Cogburn accepts the assignment and is joined by La Boeuf (Glen Campbell), a young Texas Ranger who is out to get Chaney on another charge. When they set out on their journey, Mattie tags along. The three manage to spend most of their time insulting one another, but in a series of comic and melodramatic adventures, they succeed in routing and killing off the villains. (La Boeuf dies bravely in the attempt.)

The film has many amusing, lively and suspenseful touches which give Wayne the chance to engage in some traditional heroics while keeping the full, heady flavor of a ripe characterization. One scene is his classic encounter with outlaw Ned Pepper (Robert Duvall) and his gang. Taunted by Pepper as a "one-eyed fat man," Cogburn shouts "Fill your hand, you son-of-a-bitch!" and, putting his horse's reins in his mouth, cocks his rifle with one hand and his pistol with the other and starts riding full tilt at the gang. Even at the film's

TRUE GRIT (1969). With Kim Darby

TRUE GRIT (1969). As Rooster Cogburn

G-13-26-2

end, Rooster, still feeling his oats, leaps his horse over a fence and rides off.

Directed by Henry Hathaway, *True Grit* was beautifully photographed in Technicolor and Panavision by Lucien Ballard in strikingly picturesque locations in Colorado and California. Elmer Bernstein contributed a jaunty, melodic score that added to the film's success.

William Wolf of *Cue Magazine*, not always the kindest of reviewers, said of Wayne's performance: "When the John Wayne retrospectives are in full swing, this will loom as one of his finest movie triumphs. Wayne steals the film in the role of the tough, colorful Rooster Cogburn." Most of his fans agreed, as did the membership of the Academy of Motion Picture Arts and Sciences when they gave Wayne an Academy Award, his first, as Best Actor of the Year.

A good many actors might have tossed in the career towel after doing a masterful film like *True Grit*, wanting to finish up on a high note, but Wayne shows no signs of letting up. He is working harder than ever, and only time will show us if a role as outstanding as Rooster Cogburn lies somewhere in the future.

Wayne has often stated to interviewers that he has probably made more "rotten" movies than any other actor in Hollywood. He is referring mainly to the thirties when he labored ceaselessly in low-budget features trying to make a reputation for himself and achieve some degree of stardom. His harsh self-evaluation is based partly on his memories of the long hours of backbreaking work involved in making more than sixty films, and partly with personal bitterness that he had an early chance at stardom but was denied it by a studio that failed to exploit him properly. His judgment, however, is not altogether true. Compared to expensive features, his efforts may have appeared slight, but judged against similarly produced films made under equal budgetary restrictions, his work generally stands up rather well.

Looking objectively at these early films, one must conclude that Wayne simply wasn't ready for stardom. He had a lot to learn about screen technique. His movements were awkward, his speech unmodulated and unconvincing and he revealed a demeanor that was obviously amateurish. He did, however, possess good looks, abundant athletic ability and an apparently limitless amount of energy, combined with the willingness to work hard and learn. The effort paid off well in the long run, for when stardom did

THE THIRTIES: A TEST OF ENDURANCE

beckon in the forties, he was ready and able to meet the challenge. There's an actor's expression which sums up Wayne's labors rather neatly: "He paid his dues."

Wayne generally enjoyed himself in those days when he was moving props and doing stunt work for John Ford, and getting a chance to mingle personally with all his screen heroes on the Fox lot. He gave little thought to a possible screen career until Ford gave him bit parts in *Mother Machree* and *Hangman's House*, two Irish-oriented silent films released in 1928. Happy with Wayne's work, the director gave him a larger role in *Salute*, a football story involving rivalry between Army and Navy. Before long, Wayne was making brief appearances in other Fox programmers like *Words and Music* (a musical), *Men Without Women* (a submarine story), and *Rough Romance* (an outdoor adventure).

It was at this point in his career that director Raoul Walsh selected Wayne to star in his Western adventure, *The Big Trail*. Filmed in a 70mm process called Grandeur, the film turned out to be one of the most impressive and spectacular West-

On the set of MEN WITHOUT WOMEN (1930). John Ford at the megaphone, extra John Wayne behind him

erns ever made. Highlights of the film included a realistically staged Indian attack on an encircled wagon train, an awe-inspiring buffalo hunt and chase, and panoramic displays of the pioneers encountering and overcoming natural hazards on their hazardous trek westward. Unfortunately, only a few theaters were equipped with the costly machinery to show the film in its original wide-screen format, so most audiences saw a more restrained 35mm version that tended to diminish the film's impact. *The Big Trail* had a relatively routine plot and Wayne, though doing a fairly laudable job in his first major role, could hardly compete with the acting skill of his co-stars, Ian Keith, Tully Marshall, Tyrone Power, Sr., and Marguerite Churchill. However, he did show promise and the studio, with even a modicum of foresight, should have seen that their leading man was potentially a viable acting talent.

However, instead of putting Wayne into rugged adventure

stories, the Fox moguls cast him in two lightweight bits of fluff. In *Girls Demand Excitement* Wayne was a participant in a battle between girls and boys at a co-ed school, the highlight of which was a basketball game pitting the sexes against each other. Wayne was to remember that film as very likely the worst in his career. *Three Girls Lost* wasn't much better, with its trite tale of three young women coming to the big city in search of fame and finding conflict. Wayne, annoyed and disheartened, decided he wanted out and the studio let his option drop.

Moving over to Columbia, he hoped that Harry Cohn, the despotic head of the growing company,

would give him roles more to his liking. Wayne struck out again, this time finding himself cast in supporting roles in films with titles like *Men Are Like That* (also called *Arizona*), in which he was a West Point graduate who pursued his girl from New York to a remote army post in Arizona, and *Maker of Men*, in which he was at least type-cast as a football player. The only real excitement he had at Columbia was appearing in Westerns with a couple of his early screen idols. In *Range Feud*, with Buck Jones top-billed, Wayne was the son of a rancher accused of a killing. *Texas Cyclone* and *Two-Fisted Law*, both starring Tim

THE BIG TRAIL (1930). With Tyrone Power, Sr.

McCoy, found Wayne playing young but generally ineffectual cowboy roles. It clearly was time to try his luck at another studio.

During the twenties, one of the most durable staples of the Saturday matinee theaters was the serial, a film composed of twelve or more episodes shown at the rate of one per week. Each episode ended with the hero facing some perilous situation that made audiences want to come back the following week to see how he extricated himself. It was a "hook" theater owners used to build up repeat business and was very successful. Unfortunately, the serial began to decline in popularity as talking pictures were coming into vogue and was not to regain its appeal until the late thirties and early forties. Mascot and Universal were the only two studios still making the genre when Wayne came begging and the young actor settled for the lesser of the pair, Mascot, to enter into serial production. He made three serials in all, and was one of only a few serial performers who went on to stardom. George Brent, Jennifer Jones and Carole Landis were the others.

In *Shadow of the Eagle* Wayne played a clever stunt pilot and skywriter who helped track down a mysterious criminal called "the Eagle" who was terrorizing a large corporation. There were outlandish sequences in the film in which a little toy plane wrote warning messages in the sky. (Good miniature work was not yet one of Mascot's skills.) In *Hurricane Express* the villain, known as "the Wrecker," was causing friction between a railroad and an air transport line. Wayne, still playing a pilot, finally helped track down the elusive criminal after twelve adventure-filled weeks. In his final serial, *The Three Musketeers*, Wayne was still firmly ensconced in the cockpit of an old biplane as he helped three Foreign Legionnaires track down a mysterious desert rebel known only as "El Shaitan," who was terrorizing the populace. The only virtues of appearing in the serials were that his face was kept before the public for an extended period of time, and he was given the chance to display his athletic abilities. It also offered him the opportunity to work with Yakima Canutt, an ex-rodeo-rider-turned-stuntman who would teach Wayne many valuable acting tricks.

His serial duty over, Wayne now continued his nomadic wanderings over to Warner Bros. where he was featured in a series of six entertaining but scarcely innovative B-Westerns. The films, *Haunted Gold, Ride Him, Cowboy, The Big Stampede, The Telegraph Trail, Somewhere in Sonora* and *The Man from Monterey*, were quickly filmed efforts (usually four to eight days) combining new footage largely shot

THREE GIRLS LOST (1931). With Loretta Young

THE THREE MUSKETEERS (1933). Wayne foils Robert Frazer

HAUNTED GOLD (1932). Wayne about to leap on his horse

BLUE STEEL (1934). With Eleanor Hunt

in the studio with intercut clips of impressive stock footage lifted out of silent Ken Maynard films made in the twenties. The resultant work was disjointed and unprofessional, but youthful audiences couldn't have cared less. More to humor their new Western star than anything else, they also let him play small roles in several of their more ambitious productions, such as *Central Airport* (directed by William Wellman who later did Wayne's very successful *The High and the Mighty* and the less successful *Island in the Sky* and *Blood Alley*), *Baby Face* (with Barbara Stanwyck), *The Life of Jimmy Dolan* (with Douglas Fairbanks, Jr.), and *College Coach* (with Dick Powell). He appeared to be heading down another dead-end road.

In between jobs at Columbia and Warners, he had managed to squeeze in roles as a young prizefighter in *Lady and Gent* at Paramount and as a struggling young businessman with a yen for beautiful girls in the independently released *His Private Secretary*. The continual shifting of bases of operation finally wore him down and he signed to make a series of eight B-Westerns for Monogram Pictures in 1934. With titles like *Blue Steel*, *Lucky Texan* and *Riders of Destiny*, one film was very much like the next. Most of them were both written and directed by the father of cowboy star Bob Steele, Robert N. Bradbury. In one of the films, *Randy Rides Alone*, he played a singing cowboy (with someone else dubbing in the voice), becoming one of the first of a group of Western actors who would warble and strum their way to stardom.

The initial series of eight Westerns was so successful that Wayne signed to make another eight in 1935. All sixteen films were labeled Lone Star Westerns and included such interchangeable titles as *The Dawn Rider*, *Lawless Frontier* and *Rainbow Valley*.

It was while making these Lone Star Westerns that Wayne and Yakima Canutt helped develop a more dramatic style of screen brawling. Formerly, stars like Ken Maynard, Bob Steele and others would stage their fight sequences realistically, making them wildly swinging affairs with little punches and jabs flailing indiscriminately in all directions. Wayne and Canutt perfected the long punch and follow-through (with a smack dubbed in on the sound track) that looked so much more effective and is the style still used today. Canutt, an expert horseman, also taught Wayne riding tricks which helped the younger man look more professional in the saddle.

The recently formed Republic Pictures Corporation had the next call on Wayne's services, and in 1936 he made another series of eight Westerns. Republic had a little more expertise in their production staff, and titles like *King of the Pecos*, *The Oregon Trail*, *The Lawless Nineties* and *Winds of the Wasteland* were slickly done efforts. The camerawork was first-rate, the exterior locations colorful and the acting better than average. There was also extensive use of background scoring, a feature almost totally lacking in the earlier films.

In 1937 Wayne temporarily eschewed Westerns and went over to Universal where he made a series of six minor action films that were very well received by the public. *The Sea Spoilers* found Wayne working for the Coast Guard and breaking up a gang of smugglers and animal poachers; in *Conflict* he was a lumberjack involved in fixed prizefights until Jean Rogers set him straight; *California Straight Ahead* pictured Wayne as a truckdriver involved in a race to deliver aviation parts to a waiting ship on the West Coast; *I Cover the War*, probably the best of the six films, had Wayne playing a newsreel cameraman involved in getting footage of desert rulers and finding himself up to his neck in gun-running and spies; *Idol of the Crowds*, with Wayne playing a good

CONFLICT (1936)
With Jean Rogers

skate in a hockey story and, finally, *Adventure's End* wherein pearl-diver Wayne helped prevent a mutiny aboard a whaling ship. At the very least the six films brought the young star a welcome change of pace from his saddle chores. The respite was short-lived. As soon as he left Universal he went right to Paramount where he was featured in *Born to the West* (also called *Hell Town*) with fellow cowboy actor John Mack Brown in a story based on a Zane Grey novel.

One of the most popular series of B-Westerns ever made were the Three Mesquiteer adventures turned out by Republic since 1936. The original trio featured Robert Livingston, Ray Corrigan and Max Terhune. When the studio took Livingston out in the hope of using him in more important straight features, Wayne was brought in as a substitute. His personality brought a new vigor to the series and the eight titles he appeared in were among the very best in the entire long string of Mesquiteer adventures. Titles like *Pals of the Saddle*, *Overland Stage Raiders*, *Santa Fe Stampede* and *Wyoming Outlaw* packed young fans into the Saturday "scratch houses" during 1938 and 1939.

It was while Wayne was in the middle of production on this series that the call came from his good friend John Ford to play the Ringo Kid in *Stagecoach*. When he completed his career-making loan-out assignment, he returned to finish the Mesquiteer series and bid a last goodbye to low-budget work for all time. His bosses at Republic screened *Stagecoach* and found it boring compared to their fast-action quickies, but they were in a small, blind minority this time, and unlike the Fox executives who had botched Wayne's career ten years earlier, they had no further control over the actor's future.

Wayne's pairing with Claire Trevor in *Stagecoach* had produced such good response from viewers that RKO brought them together in a frontiersman-versus-Indian adventure called *Allegheny Uprising* (1939). It was to be his final film of the thirties and he looked optimistically toward the new decade which he hoped would finally bring him stardom. It did.

PALS OF THE SADDLE (1938). With Doreen McKay and Frank Milan

ALLEGHENY UPRISING (1939). Wayne restrains Moroni Olsen from striking George Sanders. The girl: Claire Trevor

Shorn of his B-film image, Wayne plunged into his productions of the forties with vigor and enthusiasm. His pace was almost as strenuous in the next ten years as it had been in the previous ten. He made a total of thirty-two major productions, more than half of which were Westerns. Wayne now began to polish and perfect all the actor's "tricks" we now associate with him so strongly: the stylized walk as he entered into one showdown after another; clenching his teeth when angered; tucking his chin into his neck and sporting a sheepish, cow-eyed look when being admonished by someone, and the wide-eyed, almost mugging, look of surprise when receiving an unexpected punch from an antagonist. To this day, these personal gimmicks and mannerisms still turn up in virtually every new Wayne film.

Wayne was also beginning to acquire his reputation as the screen's leading portrayer of the ideal Western hero. It was an image composed of both personal and artificial ingredients. Most important of all, he looked the part. He was tall, lean, fast with a gun, a good horseman and usually excellently costumed. Moviegoers almost never saw him with his pants tucked into his boots like other cowboys; he always wore neatly tailored trousers and beautifully styled shirts. He had also learned to act and in his deportment and attitude he personified virtues

THE FORTIES: A KALEIDOSCOPE OF ACTION

we expected from our heroes: honesty, sincerity, loyalty, rugged determination and courage, all touched with compassion.

In the forties Wayne also became the screen's leading American war hero. It is amazing that he acquired this reputation considering that he made only four important films on the subject during World War II, and it wasn't until 1949 that he made his best war film. Nevertheless, the actor was now a full-fledged star, and his films were drawing large audiences. It wasn't at all unusual to see reissues of his earlier films playing concurrently with newer releases. At one point in time he had as many as eight films playing simultaneously around the country.

Wayne's long-term deal with Republic allowed him a great deal of flexibility, and he appeared in the major releases of a number of studios. Over at Universal he made a successful trio of action films with sultry beauty Marlene Dietrich whose screen image was rowdier and much less aloof after *Destry Rides Again* (1939). The first of these, *Seven Sinners* (1940), named after the saloon in which most of the action takes place, involved Dietrich as a woman of shady reputation who was continually being expelled from one island after another until she wound up on Boni-Komba. Wayne played a naval officer who found her enchanting, but who was eventually convinced that his career was more important than a hasty love affair. Dietrich stole the show this time with songs like "The Man's in the Navy" and "I've Been in Love Before," but Wayne had a great fight scene that was one of the wildest brawls ever staged. With people being thrown through mirrors, swinging from chandeliers, falling off balconies and otherwise being hurled about a barroom, the sequence has served as a model for other screen donnybrooks. Wayne was to engage in numerous fights in later films, but none ever came up to this original, directed by Tay Garnett and featuring stuntmen David Sharpe and Duke Green, among others. The main title music for *Seven Sinners*, written by Frank Skinner, was so popular that Universal used it almost constantly in a long string of action films in the forties.

The second film in the series, *The Spoilers* (1942), was the team's best match-up, and Randolph Scott was added to make it even better. *The Spoilers* had already been made three times before (in 1913-14 with

SEVEN SINNERS (1940). With Marlene Dietrich

Tom Santschi and William Farnum, in 1923 with Milton Sills and Noah Beery and in 1930 with Gary Cooper and William "Stage" Boyd), and its durable plot was well-suited to please audiences. (The film would be made a fifth time in 1955 with Rory Calhoun and Jeff Chandler). In this version of the story by Rex Beach, scenarists Lawrence Hazard and Tom Reed had Scott playing Alex McNamara, the unscrupulous gold commissioner out to "legally" steal the gold claim of Roy Glennister (Wayne) and his partner Al Dextry (Harry Carey, Sr.). The third corner of a romantic triangle with Scott and Wayne was filled by Dietrich as saloon owner Cherry Mallotte.

All the plot contrivances were only a buildup to the film's spectacular climax, a bruising barroom brawl between Wayne and Scott that justly deserves the title of "classic." Lasting several minutes, the fight begins upstairs, works its way down and all over the saloon floor and winds up on the mud-soaked streets. The actors did much of their own closeup work, and long shots of stuntmen Alan Pomeroy and Eddie Parker were cut in for the more dangerous stunts. The only flaw in the sequence is that the long shots were undercranked and move too fast to be realistic. An exciting train-wreck sequence further livened things up. Director Ray En-

right tried to activate the long dormant career of former leading man Richard Barthelmess by giving him an important role as the Bronco Kid, Dietrich's chief faro dealer, but it turned out to be only a one-shot affair.

The box-office success of The Spoilers pleased Universal, and the studio quickly reteamed the trio of stars the same year in what they hoped would be another successful adventure. But Pittsburgh missed the mark. This time Wayne was cast as the villain and Scott ended up with Dietrich. Wayne and Scott played coalminers who connive their way into becoming partners in a gigantic company. When Wayne turns greedy, Scott breaks away from him and marries Dietrich, whom both men had loved in their earlier mining days. Wayne begins to double-cross his union workers, and Scott confronts him in a mine tunnel where they stage a shorter and less exciting repeat of their brawl in The Spoilers. Everyone is forgiving in the end, and they all agree to help each other during the war years. The film was poorly scripted and generated little sympathy for the characters. One serious flaw in the film was the highly improbable and constant repetition of the theme song, "A Garden in the Rain," wherever the stars happened to be. The Spoilers and Pittsburgh were brought back con-

THE SPOILERS (1942). With Randolph Scott

tinually on a double bill all through the forties, making good money for Universal on each occasion.

Wayne's screen image as a heroic figure has seldom been challenged by "bad guy" roles, but in the forties he made two films in which he not only was a villain, but, in the end, a *dead* villain. Oddly enough, in each case it was a sea story and his demise occurred as a diver going down to destruction in the hull of a sunken ship. The first was Cecil B. DeMille's sea drama, *Reap the Wild Wind* (1942). Filmed in richly hued Technicolor, the film featured an impressive cast headed by Ray Milland, Paulette Goddard, Robert Preston, Raymond Massey and Susan Hayward. Wayne is the skipper of a ship he purposely sinks in order to gain profits from salvager Massey, after Milland has stolen Goddard away from him. Unfortunately, Susan Hayward happens to be aboard the ship and Wayne is accused of murder. At the dramatic trial Milland and Wayne agree to dive to the hull of the scuttled ship to see if Hayward is really aboard. Wayne is ordered to kill Milland when they get below, but he becomes a hero by rescuing Milland from the tentacles of a giant squid. Wayne does not escape, however, and the hull, which was perched precariously on the edge of a reef, carries him to his doom. It was imaginative, glossy entertainment in

DeMille's traditional style. The highlights were the special effects of the wrecks of the old schooners and the realistically designed squid (which remained unequaled until Disney came up with a better one in *Twenty Thousand Leagues Under the Sea*). When the film was reissued in the late fifties, Milland, who originally had top billing, was replaced by Wayne in the advertising credits.

Wake of the Red Witch (1948), Wayne's second sea story, was a much darker film. In a screenplay by Harry Brown and Kenneth Gamet, based on the book of the same title by Garland Roark, Wayne was a moody psychotic given to uncontrollable fits of rage. After complicated plot maneuvers in which Wayne received very little sympathetic treatment, he dives to recover a fortune in gold bullion that was aboard the sunken hull of the *Red Witch*, a ship he had scuttled himself earlier in the film. There was no squid this time—only the ghostly wreck slipping off the precipitous reef and taking Wayne once again to destruction. The story itself was much too confusing to qualify as good entertainment, but the special effects by Howard and Theodore Lydecker, superior to those in *Reap the Wild Wind*, at least added some degree of excitement.

Occasionally during the forties,

78

PITTSBURGH (1942). With Randolph Scott

REAP THE WILD WIND (1942). With Ray Milland, Lynne Overman, and Paulette Goddard

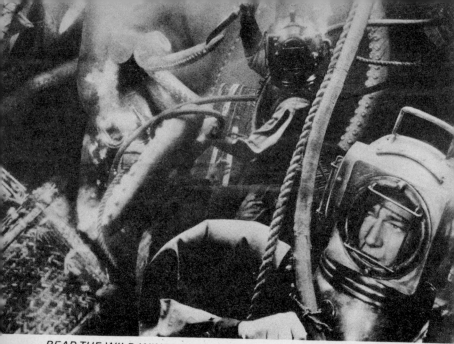

REAP THE WILD WIND (1942). With Ray Milland and the giant squid

WAKE OF THE RED WITCH (1948). With Gail Russell .

Wayne took a respite from heavy drama and hard-breathing melodrama to play comedy. The actor was much too forceful a personality to play lightweight comedy roles that demanded consistent clowning, but he did appear in two wafer-thin farces. *A Lady Takes a Chance* (1943) was the better of the two largely because Jean Arthur was his co-star. Arthur had played screwball comedy with proficiency for some years, and she provided perfect counterpoint to Wayne's awkwardness. In the film Arthur was a bank clerk who saved her money to make a bus trip out West. When the bus reaches Oregon she meets Wayne at a rodeo. (He is dumped off his horse right into her lap.) In a night of madcap fun with Wayne she inadvertently misses her bus. The remainder of the film is spent with Arthur joining Wayne and Charles Winninger in a comical journey to catch up with her tour bus. In the meantime she falls in love with the lanky cowboy and all ends happily when Wayne bodily deters some other would-be suitors.

The second film was frail but mildly amusing. In *Without Reser-*

A LADY TAKES A CHANCE (1943). With Jean Arthur

WITHOUT RESERVATIONS (1946). With Claudette Colbert

vations (1946) Claudette Colbert was a well-known authoress who meets up with Wayne and Don De-Fore on a train headed toward Hollywood. Wayne pans her work, not knowing who she is, and she becomes interested in the pair. At a stopover in Chicago she boards their train without making a reservation, and many comic situations develop. When she is thrown off the train, her male cohorts join her in further merriment as they continue their journey by auto. When Wayne finds out who she really is, he returns to his Marine base in San Diego to sulk, but eventually is reunited with Colbert and everything ends on another happy note. Wisely, Wayne left comedy alone until *The Quiet Man* came along six years later.

One of Wayne's most unusual and convincing roles was that of Ole Olson in John Ford's production of *The Long Voyage Home* (1940). Because we are so used to

Wayne's stylized manner of speech, it is a little difficult for today's film-goers to accept his broad Swedish accent, but on the film's initial release in 1940 it was considered very successful. The story was based on a series of one-act plays by Eugene O'Neill, and its stage origins are very apparent. A group of men (largely composed of Ford's "stock company" including Ward Bond, Thomas Mitchell, Barry Fitzgerald, Arthur Shields and John Qualen) sail aboard the *Glencairn* for London with a cargo of high explosives. On the long journey hostility among the men erupts into violence, until the ship is attacked by enemy planes. Some members of the crew are killed, but the ship and the sur-vivors make it to their destination. Wayne is almost shanghaied, but Mitchell rescues him and winds up being captured and brought aboard another vessel, the *Amindra*. At the film's close we see a newspaper floating in the sea which an-nounces that the *Amindra* has been sunk with all aboard lost. The moodiness and claustrophobic at-mosphere were well maintained throughout, and O'Neill was quoted as saying that he enjoyed this film version of his work more than any other adapted from his plays. It also marked Wayne's last attempt to use an accent that wasn't his own.

Everyone is entitled to at least one disaster in a decade of work. Wayne's albatross was the 1947

THE LONG VOYAGE HOME (1940). With Barry Fitzgerald and John Qualen

production of *Tycoon*. Film critic James Agee summed up this film well with a one-sentence remark which implied that several tons of dynamite went off in the movie—all under the wrong people. Never was Wayne in a more pretentious, more posturing film. Directed by Richard Wallace, who never did another Wayne movie, *Tycoon* centered on a love affair between Wayne, a railroad builder, and Laraine Day, the daughter of an industrial tycoon (Sir Cedric Hardwicke). Every time Wayne and Day would get together, Papa Hardwicke would find some way to wrench them apart. One particularly ludicrous scene had the couple running from a thunderstorm and winding up in the most artificially designed set imaginable. It was a shame, for the film did have some good action possibilities in the perils encountered building a tunnel and then a bridge, but even most of those scenes used glossy studio sets. Completely wasted were supporting players like Wayne's good friends Ward Bond and Paul Fix, as well as Anthony Quinn (who was wasted in most of his early films) and Judith Ander-

TYCOON (1947). With Sir Cedric Hardwicke

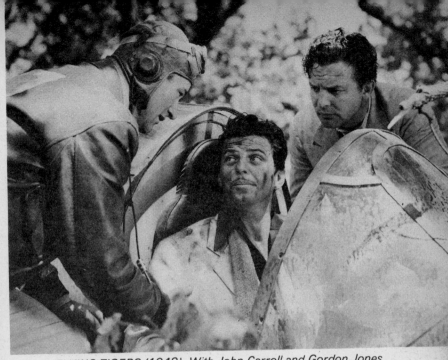
FLYING TIGERS (1942). With John Carroll and Gordon Jones

son. It was over two hours of lavish bad taste, featuring a mugging performance Wayne would like to forget.

The role of Stryker in *Sands of Iwo Jima* was Wayne's most sharply focused and realistic portrayal of a World War II fighting man, and it earned him his first Academy Award nomination, but it was not the performance which earned him the reputation as America's greatest war hero—on the screen. That image was acquired from a composite picture formed by more unrealistic portrayals in earlier films actually produced during the war years.

Wayne's two largest commercial successes were a pair of lively Republic presentations, *Flying Tigers* (1942) and *The Fighting Seabees* (1944). In the former Wayne was the heroic commander of a platoon of The American Volunteer Group, best known as "The Flying Tigers" because of fangs painted on the fuselages of their P-40 planes, who help the Chinese in their fight against the Japanese. Into his outfit comes a rebel pilot (John Carroll) who is only interested in the bounties paid for downing enemy planes and cares little for people or rules. His transgressions eventually cause the death of

Wayne's best friend (Paul Kelly) and Carroll is relieved of duty. In the climactic action, Carroll redeems himself by saving Wayne's life during a suicide mission and sacrificing his own life in the effort.

Flying Tigers was one of the most action-packed aerial thrillers turned out in the forties, though it included every cliché we associate with the genre: the American pilot gunned down as he tries to parachute to safety, the smirking enemy and the smiling Yanks, the bloodless heroic deaths of our defenders, the cowardly, blood-spattered deaths of the enemy, the "jinx" pilot who becomes a hero, the old-timer whose vision is failing and naturally winds up crashing, the wisecracking know-it-all who nearly gets everyone killed, and the rock-hard commander who is forced to make all the decisions. The film's real performers were not the players, but the elaborate special effects created by Howard Lydecker. Although the film has many spectacular air battles, not one single P-40 was a real plane. All the combat montages were miniatures, and even the planes on the ground were only mock-ups. It was a virtuoso display of movie craftsmanship.

The special effects were equally, if not more, important in Wayne's second Republic effort, *The Fighting Seabees.* They were so central to the film that Howard Lydecker actually received a co-director's credit

THE FIGHTING SEABEES (1944). With his men

and was nominated for a Special Effects Academy Award. In *The Fighting Seabees* it was Wayne's turn to be the obstinate hardhead who continually fights authority. As the head of a battalion of construction engineers, labeled "Seabees," Wayne opposes Dennis O'Keefe who, as a navy commander, wants everything done by the rules. During the construction of a vital airfield, Wayne becomes so annoyed at snipers that he recklessly takes off after the enemy, leaving a vital base unprotected. The Japanese attack in force and O'Keefe is wounded as he and his small band try to hold the area. Wayne saves the day, though he is mortally wounded in the battle. The special-effects department at Republic actually flooded several acres of land with burning oil to create an eye-popping finale. Aside from the main body of action, there was also the mandatory romantic triangle, this time involving Wayne, O'Keefe and Susan Hayward.

Wayne's other war films were meritorious, with the exception of *Reunion in France* (1942) in which he had a lesser role as a downed RAF pilot involved with the French underground. In *Back to Bataan* (1945) Wayne and Anthony Quinn helped organize a guerrilla force to help liberate the islands from the Japanese, and in *They Were Expendable* (1945) Robert Montgomery was Wayne's companion in

THEY WERE EXPENDABLE (1945). With Donna Reed and Robert Montgomery

DARK COMMAND (1940). With Claire Trevor and Roy Rogers

heroics as they played a couple of PT boat skippers who seemed to single-handedly win the war in the Philippines for America. It was lively entertainment but it offered the kind of mindless heroics that young people were to berate Wayne for in later years. Nevertheless, the films were important morale-boosters for those at home, and that was the principal reason for their being made.

Wayne's outstanding performances in *Red River* and *She Wore a Yellow Ribbon* in the late forties topped a long string of well-done and commercially successful Western films produced during the decade. Lesser films like *Three Faces West* (1940), *Lady from Louisiana* (1941), *Lady For a Night* (1941), and *A Man Betrayed* (1941), turgid costume dramas rather than Westerns, kept Wayne steadily working at Republic, but did little for his career. The studio had started off on the right foot in 1940 with their sprawling production of *Dark Com-*

mand (1940). As Wayne's first film of the forties, *Dark Command* found him in conflict with Walter Pidgeon. Pidgeon played William Cantrell, leader of a ruthless band of renegades who were riding and pillaging the country around Lawrence, Kansas during the Civil War. Ordinarily budget-minded, Republic pulled out all the stops by using a large cast of players and by staging a finale which involved almost an entire town being burned to the ground. In addition to Wayne, Pidgeon, and Claire Trevor, the studio also added roles for its rapidly rising B-Western star team, Roy Rogers and George "Gabby" Hayes, who turned in most creditable jobs.

Between Republic assignments Wayne went over to Paramount where he appeared with Betty Field, Harry Carey, Sr. and Beulah Bondi in his first Technicolor film, *The Shepherd of the Hills* (1941). As a young mountaineer vengefully seeking his father who he felt had betrayed his mother, Wayne gave a first-class, though occasionally awkward performance.

Wayne's role in *In Old California* (1942), made back at Republic, would have given his father some pleasure had the elder Morrison lived to see his son's success. (He died prior to Wayne's appearance in *Stagecoach*.) He played a young pharmacist who traveled West to set up his own apothecary shop. Opposing him was Albert Dekker who was annoyed because he felt his girlfriend (Binnie Barnes) was falling for the young druggist. After many attempts to discredit Wayne, including putting poison in some of his prescriptions, Dekker is finally uncovered as a villain. Wayne endears himself to the populace by helping them during a fever epidemic and all ends well in a typical combination of action, violence and love, Republic-style.

Albert Dekker was back after Wayne's blood in 1943's *In Old Oklahoma* (also called *War of the Wildcats*), a rousing tale of men fighting for control of rich Indian-owned oil fields. The film's dramatic finale found Wayne racing dozens of oil-laden wagons through blazing fields in order to make a deadline at a Tulsa refinery. The stunt shots of wagons exploding, turning over and plunging off cliffs were genuinely exciting. Every Wayne film had to have a slugfest in it and Wayne and Dekker's battle in *In Old California* was brutal and acrobatic.

Having successfully bested Dekker twice, Wayne now took on his old friend Ward Bond in a couple of solid entries: *Tall in the Saddle* (1944) and *Dakota* (1945). In the former Wayne was involved in a tale of murder over stolen land and a tangled romantic triangle involving him with Audrey Long and Ella

TALL IN THE SADDLE (1944). With Ward Bond

Raines. The screenplay by Michael Hogan and Paul J. Fix was complicated, but it gave Wayne and his fellow actors a chance to display more acting ability than usual. Again, a highlight was a slam-bang battle between leads Wayne and Bond. Some welcome comedy relief was supplied by George "Gabby" Hayes. *Tall in the Saddle*, released by RKO, offered one of Wayne's most mature and intelligent Western portrayals.

In contrast, *Dakota* matched Wayne and Bond in a light-handed action piece about a land-hungry gang leader (Bond) who was trying to force out farmers by destroying their property and burning their wheat crops. Naturally Wayne upset Bond's plan. Wayne's most imposing challenge in the movie was working with Vera Hruba Ralston, the wife of Republic's head man, Herbert J. Yates. Yates kept casting his wife in important films, earning the enmity of fans and stockholders alike. She could be considered, at best, Wayne's least effective leading lady in his long

ANGEL AND THE BADMAN (1947). With Harry Carey and Gail Russell

career of major films.

In 1947 Wayne became one of the first major stars to become a producer. He was anxious to exert greater control over his selection of roles and the quality of production as well as to increase the profit on his own work. His first production, released through Republic, was a film that pleased both him and his fans: *Angel and the Badman* (1947). Written by James Edward Grant, it had Wayne as gunman Quirt Evans who is wounded fleeing from a posse and finds refuge with a family of Quakers. While building up his strength, he falls in love with Prudence (Gail Russell). Quirt has vowed to kill Laredo Stevens (Bruce Cabot) who is responsible for the death of his foster-father. After repeated episodes of violence, Quirt goes to meet Laredo in a showdown. Prudence rides to town and convinces Quirt to give up his gun for both their sakes. When Laredo is about to gun down Quirt, he is himself killed by Marshal McClintock (Harry Carey, Sr.) who has been on Quirt's trail. The film had many moments of tenderness and compassion, that underscored the surrounding mayhem. Wayne's subsequent production under his newly formed production arm was the undistinguished *The Fighting Kentuckian* (1949) which once again gave him the handicap of Vera Ralston as his co-star. The only virtue of the film was a solo appearance by Oliver Hardy (without partner Stan Laurel) in a comedy role.

Wayne's final Western appearances in the forties were in two exceptionally well done John Ford films: *Fort Apache* (1945) and *Three Godfathers* (1948). In *Fort Apache* Wayne's main battle was with Henry Fonda more than the Indians. As Lt. Col. Thursday, Fonda was sent from the East to take command of Fort Apache. Demoted from the rank of general, he now seeks only to restore his reputation. Completely inexperienced in Indian-fighting, Fonda earns the animosity of his men, especially Captain York (Wayne). The friction both from outside and inside the fort builds as Fonda's daughter falls

FORT APACHE (1948). With Shirley Temple, Anna Lee, George O'Brien and John Agar

in love with one of his young officers and the Indians become an increasing threat. Fonda finally orders a completely misguided and foolhardy attack against Cochise and his band of Apaches. The Indians manage to destroy Fonda and his troop, allowing only Wayne to return with a few men to the fort. Wayne, in a noble gesture, obviates Fonda's stupidity by covering up for him. Wayne gave a very effective performance and was singled out by Bosley Crowther in his *Times* review: "John Wayne is powerful, forthright and exquisitely brave." The film, adapted by Frank S. Nugent from a story in the *Saturday Evening Post*, was stunningly photographed in black and white by A.J. Stout. In addition to Wayne and Fonda, the large cast included Shirley Temple (as Fonda's daughter), John Agar, Pedro Armendariz, Ward Bond, George O'Brien and Victor McLaglen. If Wayne's performance seems somewhat diminished in *Fort Apache*, it is only because Fonda's was so much stronger and persuasive.

The second Ford film, *Three Godfathers*, was derived from the Peter B. Kyne story that had been filmed several times before. Its simple tale of three bank robbers who find and protect an infant as they flee across the desert was written this time by Laurence Stallings and Frank S. Nugent. Winton Hoch, who did most of Ford's best color work in this period, did some fine Technicolor photography, aided by Charles Boyle. The performances by the three leads, Wayne, Armendariz, and Harry Carey, Jr. were forcefully augmented by Ward Bond, Mildred Natwick, Ben Johnson and others. A touching and typically sentimental Ford touch was added when the film carried a dedication to the late Harry Carey, Sr., a good friend of the director as well as Wayne. The film drew praise from most critics. Howard Barnes in the *New York Herald Tribune* said that Wayne was "better than ever as the leader of the badmen," and Bosley Crowther in the *Times* said the star was "wonderfully raw and ructious" and that the film had "humor and honest tear-jerking." It was one of Wayne's most memorable portraits.

As the forties drew to a close, Wayne could look with a certain amount of pride at how far he had come in the decade. He entered the fifties as an established actor and a new producer who felt he could now determine the kind of pictures his audiences should see. His judgment was to be strongly put to the test.

THREE GODFATHERS (1948). As Robert Hightower

Were it not for Wayne's appearances in five first-rate Westerns and *The Quiet Man*, his career might well have come to a disappointing conclusion in the fifties. Caring little to reinforce the sturdy image he had worked so hard to achieve in the preceding decade, he decided to demonstrate his versatility in his own productions. The result was an alarming number of badly written, overacted melodramas that were not only poor, but embarrassing.

The worst offender in this melange of mediocrity was his 1952 production of *Big Jim McLain*, the first release by the Wayne-Fellows company the actor had formed with Robert Fellows. During the forties, Wayne had begun to earn a reputation as an aggressive "hawk" and the McCarthy era of witch-hunting seemed to encourage him. His virtual hatred of Communism as an ideology was given open expression at every opportunity. When he had James Edward Grant, Richard English and Eric Taylor fashion a screenplay about the subject, the result was an open assault against our intelligence. The story focused on the uncovering of a Communist plot being hatched in the Hawaiian Islands and for ninety minutes we were lectured on Americanism. The Fifth Amendment was criticized because the enemy hid behind it, and as a grim reminder of the penalty for being unprepared, we were

THE FIFTIES: PEAKS AND VALLEYS

given a tour of the graveyard of American vessels sunk on December 7, 1941, by the Japanese. Wayne, who narrated over a great deal of footage, threw in a little flag-waving whenever he possibly could. Even the main title music set up the audience, being composed of traditional pieces like "Yankee Doodle" and "Dixie." Then, with the wind howling and bolts of lightning streaking across the screen, Harry Morgan's voice rang out with quotes from *The Devil and Daniel Webster* asking us "How goes the Union?" At that moment it didn't seem to be going well at all. The advertising for the film showed Wayne with fist cocked and teeth clenched and proudly proclaimed, "Uncle Sam said 'Go Get 'Em!' . . . and Big Jim was the man they sent!" *Big Jim McLain* made even *Tycoon* look good by comparison.

The elusive billionaire, Howard Hughes, was good at making planes and money, but very bad at making films. Wayne appeared in three Hughes productions during the fifties, and the first was so bad that it was kept off theater screens for almost eight years. In *Jet Pilot* (1950), Janet Leigh played a Russian pilot

BIG JIM McLAIN (1952). With James Arness

and spy who flies to the United States to obtain information and winds up falling for Wayne. Curiously enough, the film was directed by Josef von Sternberg, who had helped guide Marlene Dietrich to fame in a group of exotic Paramount films of the thirties. The sorry concoction of bad story and terrible acting was completed in 1950, but saw the light of movie screens only in 1957. It should never have been released at all.

The second Hughes film, made a year later, fared a little better. *Flying Leathernecks* (1951) had some excellent action scenes and a powerful teaming of Wayne and Robert Ryan. As in *Sands of Iwo Jima*, Wayne was an officer who trained his men to be killers and in so doing earned their animosity. Filmed in Technicolor, which produced some very effective action footage, the script was done by James Edward Grant, Wayne's favorite writer, who drew on a story by Kenneth Gamet. Nicholas Ray capably handled the directing chores.

The final film of the threesome was one of Wayne's worst. Wayne put on an Oriental mustache and in the title role of *The Conqueror* (1956) cut a ludicrous figure as the twelfth-century Mongol leader, Temujin. He and Susan Hayward as the beautiful Tartar captive, Bortai, simply shudder when anyone even mentions this film directed by,

FLYING LEATHERNECKS (1951). With Robert Ryan

ISLAND IN THE SKY (1953). With Wally Cassell

THE HIGH AND THE MIGHTY (1954). With William Campbell

of all people, Dick Powell. Filmed in color and CinemaScope, it is a monument to bad taste.

Trouble Along the Way (1953) was a nondescript little soap opera in which Wayne played an ex-football coach who is called upon by a rector to help raise enough money to save his school from being closed down. Wayne becomes a savior when he builds a winning team for the school, and also manages to fall in love with co-star Donna Reed. The amiable but rather listless proceedings were directed by Michael Curtiz.

The next Wayne-Fellows production that surfaced through Warner Bros. was *Island in the Sky* (1953). In this airplane drama directed by

William Wellman, Wayne and his crew of civilian pilots flying for the army are forced to make a landing in an uncharted area of Labrador. The remainder of the film focuses on the crew's struggle for survival and the desperate search for the missing men by their friends. The capable cast, headed by Lloyd Nolan, Walter Abel, James Arness, Andy Devine and other reliable character actors, gave convincing performances, but the artificial sets intercut with good exteriors never made the audience feel any real sense of danger.

The following year another airplane picture, also directed by Wellman, did give Wayne's sagging career a boost. *The High and the*

THE SEA CHASE (1955). With Lana Turner

Mighty (1954), adapted by Ernest K. Gann from his popular novel, found Wayne once again playing a pilot. This time he was flying an impressive cast that included Claire Trevor, Laraine Day, Robert Stack, Jan Sterling, Phil Harris, Robert Newton, David Brian, and Paul Kelly, from Hawaii to San Francisco. During the flight we gain insights into the characters of the passengers in a series of vignettes. When a fight breaks out, a wild gunshot causes one engine of the plane to explode, placing the flight in peril. Wayne's coolness and professionalism help him bring the plane safely down at their destination. The long film had neither a new or original theme, vari-

ations of the group-in-danger plot having turned up on the screen many times before, but it was the most elaborate made to that time. The film's theme music was ubiquitous on radio and television.

In 1955 Wayne turned from planes to boats, appearing in two Warner Bros. releases that were strictly routine action fare. In *The Sea Chase* he was the commander of an outlaw freighter bound for Valparaiso with Lana Turner aboard as a passenger. In hot pursuit is David Farrar who believes Wayne machine-gunned six helpless fisherman to death on an island raid, not knowing that Lyle Bettger, Wayne's first mate, was really the guilty party. To complicate matters,

both Wayne and Bettger fall for Turner. There is a final confrontation and Farrar sinks Wayne's ship, supposedly with Wayne and Turner aboard. Turner has managed to smuggle Wayne's log aboard one lifeboat so that Farrar will know his one-time friend was innocent, and we are left wondering whether the couple really survived or not. John Farrow directed the color film slickly, but Wayne merely walked through his role.

William Wellman was in charge of Wayne's second boat trip. In 1954 Wayne had reformed his original production company and called the new organization Batjac. One of their first releases was *Blood Alley*. This time Wayne is a ship's captain in the Far East who is approached by Lauren Bacall and asked to guide

her and a group of frightened villagers to safety from communist domination by sailing an antique ferry-boat through the Formosa Straits (referred to as "Blood Alley"). He takes on the dangerous assignment and after numerous close calls and attacks by both men and planes, he safely brings the ship to Hong Kong. One particularly clever scene found Wayne covering his ship with garbage so that sea gulls in search of food land by the thousands and successfully camouflage the vessel, safely hiding it from a searching plane. Wayne and Bacall, both strong screen personalities, played well together, but the framework of the film was too fragile to offer them any real challenge. Filmed in Warnercolor and CinemaScope,

100

THE BARBARIAN AND THE GEISHA (1958).
As Townsend Harris

the film at least had the virtue of colorful scenery.

Time magazine's comment on *The Barbarian and the Geisha*, a 1958 Wayne fiasco, was succinct and apt: "Ouch—there goes three million bucks!" Director John Huston was primarily responsible for getting Wayne into this predicament. Huston had been so impressed by several Japanese-made movies that he wanted to go to Japan and do one himself. He chose the true story of Townsend Harris, the first accredited diplomatic representative to Japan from the United States in the mid-nineteenth century, and fashioned an absurd fictional tale involving, among other things, Harris' relations with a lovely geisha girl (Eiko Ando). Huston chose Wayne because of his size and toughness, believing he would stand out among the diminutive Japanese. The director and star very seldom agreed during most of the subsequent production, but Wayne couldn't turn down the $700,000 he was getting for the work (the largest amount ever paid to a star at the time). Huston, who, along with his good friend Humphrey Bogart, had never really cared for Wayne and his politics, seemed to go out of his way to make things difficult. Wayne decried the fact that the movie had almost none of the elements his fans wanted. *Newsweek* agreed, calling the film "lamentably tedious." Wayne could be heard to say kiddingly that the film, released by 20th Century-Fox, was his revenge for what the studio had done to him in those early days of the thirties.

A much more suitable role for Wayne than Townsend Harris was Commander Frank W. "Spig" Wead, whom the actor portrayed in *The Wings of Eagles* (1957). The real-life career of Commander Wead was more colorful than most screenwriters could ever concoct. A daredevil flier, author, inventor, and general bon vivant, Wead was a good friend of John Ford (he wrote the screenplays for Ford's productions of *Air Mail* and *They Were Expendable*) and the director firmly believed his biography would make a good film. He was only partly right. By underplaying many of Wead's more colorful moments, the screenplay tended to stress the more soap-opera-oriented aspects of his romance with his wife and his long recovery from the broken neck received in a fall down a flight of stairs. Wayne did the best he could, displaying courage and confidence as he faced the long journey back to health, but his scenes were offset by the scene-chewing tantrums thrown by his wife, Maureen O'Hara. One of the most talked-about roles in the film was that of Ford himself—here called "John Dodge" and played by Ward Bond.

THE WINGS OF EAGLES (1957). With Dan Dailey

The director said that it was Bond's idea and not his own, but there was enough ham in the veteran to be a little flattered by it all. The film was released in Metrocolor by MGM. Despite its shortcomings, *The Wings of Eagles* featured one of Wayne's better non-Western portrayals.

Rio Grande, directed by Ford in 1950, was the final statement in the famed cavalry trilogy and was the weakest entry. The material was first-rate, but *Fort Apache* and *She*

Wore a Yellow Ribbon were immeasurably better. In a screenplay by James Kevin McGuinness, based on a *Saturday Evening Post* story by James Warner Bellah, Wayne played Lt. Col. Kirby Yorke, who, during the Civil War, is ordered to burn down the plantation owned by his Southern wife (Maureen O'Hara), causing their long estrangement. Years later, Yorke is in charge of fighting a treacherous pack of marauding Apaches who are violating the United States pact

with Mexico by making death-dealing raids across the Rio Grande. Yorke is joined in the fight by the son he has not seen before, who is assigned to his father's cavalry troop. Yorke's wife also turns up to plead for their son's discharge. In a final battle with the Apaches, father and son are triumphant, and the family is reunited. Wayne, sporting a moustache, turned in what the *New York Herald Tribune* called "a first-rate portrayal." Supporting players included Ford regulars Ben Johnson (whose riding abilities the director marveled over constantly), Victor McLaglen, Chill Wills, Harry Carey, Jr., Grant Withers and, as Wayne's son, Claude Jarman, Jr., who had played Jody in *The Yearling*. The striking black and white photography was by Bert Glennon and A.J. Stout and contained some excellently composed exterior tableaus.

Hondo, a 1953 Wayne-Fellows production released through Warner Bros., was originally made in the three-dimensional process to cash in on the then-current vogue for eye-straining 3-D entertainments, but because CinemaScope had already begun to displace the more complicated earlier techniques, the film was released in the standard flat screen format. The screenplay by James Edward

RIO GRANDE (1959). As Lt. Col. Yorke

Grant, based on a story by Louis L'Amour, centered on the exploits of a U.S. cavalry dispatch rider called Hondo Lane, played by Wayne. The film focused on Hondo's relationship with a resilient pioneer woman (Geraldine Page), whose husband deserted her and her young son (Lee Aaker) during an Apache raid. Later, Hondo shoots a stranger in town who tries to ambush him, only to learn that he has killed the woman's husband. The script also dealt with Hondo's capture and torture by a tribe of Apaches. Admiring his bravery after a vicious knife duel, the chief of the Apaches releases Hondo, who hurries to the woman he finds he now loves and confesses that he killed her husband. Following more Indian action, the family finally heads for California and happiness. Most Wayne fans were very pleased with the film which gave the actor a good number of rugged action scenes. It was the kind of role that Wayne could jokingly say of himself, "I'll be damned if I'm not the stuff men are made of." William K.

HONDO (1953). With Geraldine Page and Lee Aaker

H-304

THE HORSE SOLDIERS (1959). With William Holden

Everson, a well-respected authority on Western films, considers *Hondo* "the best John Wayne vehicle not made by John Ford."

Wayne's final Western of the decade was another John Ford opus, *The Horse Soldiers* (1959), which teamed Wayne with William Holden. Holden was an army surgeon during the Civil War and Wayne was his argumentative superior officer. The plot line had Wayne sent by President Grant with a small body of men into enemy territory to cut railway lines. Wayne's long trek on horseback becomes a challenge which is hampered when Holden keeps declaring men unfit for duty because of injuries. To complicate matters, both men become intrigued by a fetching Southern belle (Constance Towers). The men's mission is finally accomplished only after a series of engagements with enemy forces. The climax comes when they blow up a bridge which prevents their pursuers from overtaking them. Wayne rides off into the distance, vowing to return to Towers when the war is over. Though *The Horse Soldiers*, released through United Artists, was considerably more expensive than Ford's cavalry films of a decade earlier, it was noticeably inferior in content and quality. Its most striking feature was the DeLuxe Color scenes of the mounted soldiers riding single-file and silhouetted against the sky, which were photographed by William Clothier. The screenplay for the film was conceived by John Lee Mahin and Martin Rackin from Harold Sinclair's novel.

Wayne's work in the fifties taught him one very important lesson—not to experiment too much. His fans wanted to see Wayne tall in the saddle, and he gave them Wayne lost in Japan, or Peru, or Tibet. It very nearly nipped his ascending career in the bud. In the next ten years he would give the public more of what they craved, and throw in some enjoyment for himself as well.

With his image badly tarnished by a number of poor films in the preceding decade, Wayne set about restructuring his screen work into more profitable and rewarding channels. In the next ten years he would concentrate once more on his most solidly reliable format, the Western. However, this new crop of wide-screen adventures would add a warmer, more earthy note to his traditional characterization of the heroic figure, one filled with humor, color and bravado. His earlier depictions of moody, introspective men would find expression here only in *The Man Who Shot Liberty Valance*, his last Western to date to be photographed in black and white. Although most critics would regard many of these sixties vehicles as broad satires or parodies of his solid constructions of the past, they are really humanistic portrayals of men involved in a flamboyant era. All of his sixties films in the genre contained colorful action sequences, but they were now overflowing with a broad spirit of fun and laughter which made them not only acceptable to his old fans, but a whole new generation of young filmgoers.

The sixties would also signal the achievement of two of the actor's great dreams; to make his long-planned *The Alamo*, and to win an Academy Award. Unfortunately, the years would also be marked by

THE SIXTIES: REBUILDING AN IMAGE

near-tragedy with the actor's bout with cancer, but like his movies that story had an equally happy ending.

After Wayne had invested all his money and effort into making *The Alamo* and finding the film to be less than a success commercially, he immediately set to work to recover from his fiscal dilemma by making some colorful outdoor adventures. The first of these could be called a North-Western. In *North to Alaska* (1960) Wayne and his partner Stewart Granger discover gold. Mickey Shaughnessy and his band of crooks try to steal their claim, and our heroes mop up the muddy streets with them. Interwoven in the routine plot were humorous con jobs performed by talented Ernie Kovacs, making one of his few film appearances before his untimely early death. Fabian, then one of the most popular young singers of the day, also had a good part that involved him in a romantic quadrangle with Wayne, Granger and French actress Capucine. The film was directed with zest and flair by Henry Hathaway, who kept the cast in a constant state of riotous activity.

NORTH TO ALASKA (1960). With Fabian, Stewart Granger, and Capucine

The Comancheros (1961), another pleasing and highly colorful diversion followed immediately. This time director Michael Curtiz was at the helm as he put Wayne and co-star Stuart Whitman through their paces. Wayne plays a Texas Ranger who first arrests gambler Whitman on a murder charge, then ultimately joins him in a whirlwind journey across Texas to capture a group of marauding outlaws who call themselves the Comancheros. Lee Marvin is the boozy head of a band of gunrunners smuggling guns to the Comancheros. The lively climax found Wayne and Whitman imprisoned in

the outlaw fortress, only to succeed in wiping out the terrorists through a clever plan and the timely arrival of the Rangers. It was all great fun with picturesque wagon chases through spectacularly beautiful scenic locations, well-staged Indian attacks, and a variety of exciting pyrotechnics. An impressive Elmer Bernstein score also made a valuable contribution.

After appearing in a brief cameo role as General Sherman in the Civil War sequence of *How the West Was Won* (1963) for his friend John Ford, Wayne then made one of his most entertaining films: *McLintock!* (1963). It was the first time Andrew V. McLaglen, (Victor's son), directed Wayne in a solo effort. He had worked with Wayne as early as 1953 as co-director of *Island in the Sky*, but had concentrated his efforts mainly on television series like *Have Gun, Will Travel*. The two worked well together, and McLaglen continues to be one of the actor's best directors and personal friends.

Many people tend to forget the name of the film, referring to it only as "that one with the big mud fight." The sequence was certainly the high spot of the film—a wild melee in which over a hundred stuntmen as well as co-star Maureen O'Hara found themselves being thrown down a muddy embankment and winding up being covered head to toe with mud. The story, written by James Edward Grant, involved Wayne as a rancher who was estranged from his wife (O'Hara) because she suspected him of infidelity. She returns from a two-year separation seeking a final divorce and custody of their daughter. In the meantime Wayne has hired Yvonne De Carlo as a cook, thus setting up a hectic triangle. After many comic sequences involving ranchers, Indians, townspeople and

THE COMANCHEROS (1961). With Ina Balin and Stuart Whitman

virtually everyone else the director could crowd into the film, Wayne repeats his *Quiet Man* sequence by dragging O'Hara all over town and then giving her a good spanking. It was all enjoyable to watch, and one of Wayne's most thoroughly pleasant films.

After Wayne had undergone surgery for cancer and proudly proclaimed, "I've licked the Big C," his next project after recuperation was the well-received *The Sons of Katie Elder* (1965). For a man who had just lost half a lung, it was not an easy task to complete. The film had many action sequences that de-

manded his actual participation because of necessary closeups. It was also being shot in locations that were over 7,000 feet in altitude, making breathing even more difficult than normal. Wayne was visibly straining not only to ride, but even to get on a horse. But he survived and turned in a solid performance.

Henry Hathaway directed the Technicolor film for Paramount and the screenplay by William H. Wright, Allan Weiss and Harry Essex (based on a story by Talbot Jennings) began with Wayne and his three brothers (Dean Martin, Earl

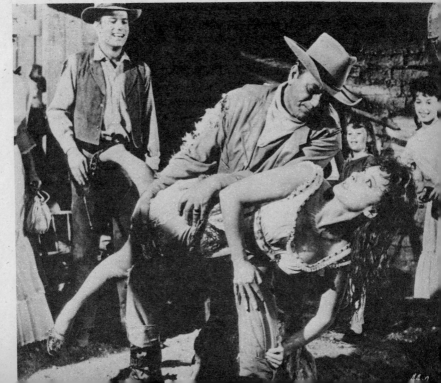

McLINTOCK! (1963). With Maureen O'Hara

111

THE SONS OF KATIE ELDER (1965). With Dean Martin

THE WAR WAGON (1967). With Kirk Douglas

Holliman and Michael Anderson, Jr.) returning to the Texas town of Clearwater to attend the funeral of their mother. While they were away, James Gregory had murdered their father and taken away their land by means of a phony bill of sale. Before they can uncover the facts, Gregory frames them for a murder and they are all locked up. After Holliman is killed in an ambush, Wayne and Martin make their way back to town and kill Gregory in a showdown. The film had some exceptional color photography by Lucien Ballard and first-rate music by Elmer Bernstein. *The Sons of Katie Elder* remains one of Wayne's most popular films, drawing high ratings when shown on television.

The same kind of color and excitement was to be found in *The War Wagon*, a 1967 Batjac production released through Universal. Wayne was paired this time with an equally strong performer, Kirk Douglas. Bruce Cabot, the villain of the story, hires Douglas to kill Wayne, but the latter talks him into joining him in a robbery scheme which will be much more profitable to them both. Cabot is shipping a large amount of money in an armor-plated stagecoach he calls "The War Wagon," and Wayne and Douglas, joined by Howard Keel, Robert Walker and Keenan Wynn, are going to steal the money in a cleverly conceived scheme. Their plot is successful, but a tribe of Indians attacks them and makes off with most of the loot. Enough money remains to make it all worthwhile. There was a lot of laughter in the byplay between Wayne and Douglas, particularly in a raucous barroom brawl involving not only the leads but everyone in the room. Burt Kennedy, another skillful director of action films, was in charge this time around and Dimitri Tiomkin, who hadn't done much work in films in the sixties, wrote the background score.

El Dorado (1967), a Paramount release, was a case of Hawks reworking Hawks. The plot of *El Dorado* was almost a carbon copy of *Rio Bravo*. Wayne was playing his identical role as town marshal, Robert Mitchum was standing in for Dean Martin, James Caan for Ricky Nelson and Arthur Hunnicutt replaced Walter Brennan. As in *Rio Bravo*, most of the action centered on the town jail with a gang of determined cutthroats bent on blasting the lawmen from the building.

EL DORADO (1967). With Edward Asner

THE UNDEFEATED (1969). With Rock Hudson

Several new gimmicks were thrown in this time to add interest: Wayne was shot and wounded earlier and as a result finds his gun arm becoming paralyzed at very inappropriate times, Caan was a knife-thrower rather than a gunfighter, and Mitchum is not only a drunk but a comical one at that. A lot of footage was taken up by scenes such as the one in which Wayne, Caan and Hunnicutt try to sober Mitchum up by pouring a filthy concoction down his throat. It's almost as if we were back in the days of the Keystone Kops as Mitchum rolls his eyes and clutches his protruding stomach in mock agony. The exciting final shoot-out was very well done, but we had seen the same scene so often

before that its effectiveness was lessened considerably. The screenplay was by Leigh Brackett (who had also written *Rio Bravo*), based to some extent on the novel *The Stars in Their Courses* by Harry Brown.

Other than *The Man Who Shot Liberty Valance*, John Ford's moody farewell to the legend of the Old West, and *True Grit*, featuring Wayne's award-winning performance as Rooster Cogburn, the actor's only remaining Western produced in the sixties was *The Undefeated* (1969). This film co-starred him with Rock Hudson in a story that gave more prominence to a huge herd of horses than to any of its human leads. Here Wayne is a horse wrangler and ex-Northern

115

Army officer who, on a trip to Mexico to sell horses, runs into the Confederate officer (Hudson) he had battled earlier in the Civil War, on his way to join up with Mexicans who are still willing to carry on the fight against the North. Both men become unwilling participants in the battle between Emperor Maximilian and Benito Juarez. General Rojas (Antonio Aguilar), working for Juarez, captures the Confederates led by Hudson and threatens to kill them all if Wayne doesn't turn over his horses to them. Wayne gives in, loses his herd and he and Hudson head back to the United States, poorer but wiser. The spectacularly graphic shots of the horse herds moving through dazzling Mexican scenery were the real high-spots of the film (photographed by William Clothier), along with the by-now mandatory free-for-all donnybrook. Wayne had able support from Ben Johnson as his sidekick and director Andrew V. McLaglen made the most of a fragile script.

Scattered among Wayne's Western portrayals were his appearances in a number of other action-oriented films that ranged in quality from reasonably good to downright poor. The best of the lot was Howard Hawks' 1962 production of *Hatari*. The story by Harry Kurnitz, fashioned into a screenplay by Leigh Brackett, portrayed Wayne as a big-game hunter in East Africa. Surrounded by an odd assortment

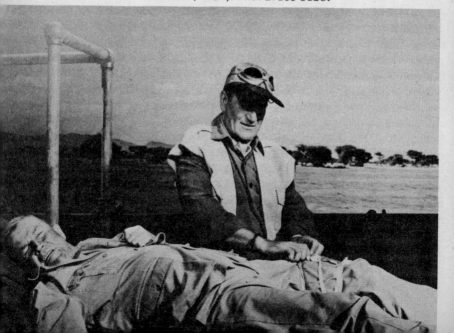

HATARI (1961). With Bruce Cabot

DONOVAN'S REEF (1963). With Lee Marvin

of co-workers, including Red Buttons and Hardy Kruger, Wayne is maintaining one of the best zoo-supplying game farms in the area. Into his close-knit little unit comes a woman photographer (Elsa Martinelli) who wants to capture Wayne's work on film. The result is a tangled web of romantic triangles, noisy bickering between the co-workers and occasional bursts of vivid action. It all works out satisfactorily, but the drama plays second fiddle to the scene-stealing animals, including some very hammy baby elephants. The most exciting sequences are, as might well be expected, the animal hunts, including a thrilling chase after rhinos. Hawks' cinematic skill was at its peak here, weaving colorful tapestries that dazzled the eyes and senses of moviegoers. A particularly gripping scene of Wayne's shooting a charging elephant was cut from the final print only because it was felt that his fans would not like to see their screen hero killing such a noble beast. The Technicolor photography by Russell Harlan is among the best that fine cameraman has ever done, and Henry Mancini composed a very commercial background score.

In *Donovan's Reef* (1963) Wayne's comical antagonist was Lee Marvin, who was finally beginning to work his way up into co-starring roles after many years of playing minor character parts. Director John Ford imbued the Technicolor film with many of the laugh-provoking ingredients of his earlier film, *The Quiet Man*. Wayne and Jack Warden are a couple of ex-navy men who stay on an island after the war where Wayne sets up a thriving bar called "Donovan's Reef." Marvin, an ex-shipmate who wants to continue his brawling friendship with Wayne, comes to the island on a visit. Into their lives steps Warden's daughter (Elizabeth Allen), seeking him out after many years. Wayne, Warden and Dorothy Lamour, playing a small part as a bar singer, plan a scheme to save Warden's somewhat tarnished reputation. After much fighting, drinking and other hectic activity, the whole affair ends happily. The film was a mixed blessing for Wayne. He loved boats—at various times he owned a few, including his yacht *The Wild Goose*—and he relished the excitement of filming in the islands. But *Donovan's Reef* also marked the last time Wayne would be directed in a film by John Ford. Ford's declining health prevented the pair from turning out any more films. Throughout the director's remaining years Wayne was his closest pal, and the actor was one of the last to see him on the final day of his life. Wayne has said that when his time comes he wants the services to be held in John Ford's small private chapel, because everything really began for him with Ford.

Circus World (1964), directed by Henry Hathaway, was an elaborate, cliché-ridden drama in which Wayne played the impresario of a Wild West show. He plans to take his troupe to Europe and, once there, hopes to find the woman he still loves, the aerialist (Rita Hayworth) who disappeared years before when her acrobat husband committed suicide over her infidelity. The woman's beautiful young daughter (Claudia Cardinale) is in love with Wayne's star performer (John Smith). After a series of tragic mishaps, Wayne and Hayworth become romantically attached, mother and daughter find each other, and their Wild West Show thrives again. The two elaborate action scenes were the only virtues of *Circus World*. In one sequence, Wayne stages a performance of aerialists aboard a ship. When one of the performers falls overboard, the entire audience rushes to the rail, and the ship capsizes, providing a chance for heroics. The other high spot was a fire sequence, in which Wayne was nearly seriously burned during filming, when their

CIRCUS WORLD (1964). A ship capsizes. Wayne to the rescue

Big Top tent catches fire. The plodding, unconvincing drama was written by Ben Hecht, Julian Halevy and James Edward Grant, based on a story by Philip Yordan and Nicholas Ray. Veteran cameraman Jack Hildyard did the photography.

Wayne made a very brief cameo appearance as a centurion who follows Jesus to the Crucifixion in George Stevens' poorly received production of *The Greatest Story Ever Told* (1965), in which he looked completely out of place. *Hellfighters* (1969) was more to his liking. In this Andrew V. McLaglen-directed drama, made just before *True Grit*, Wayne was a man who could put out oil fires. He is called to Latin America, where one

dandy of a blaze is raging. After much vigorous heroism, Wayne succeeds in ending the peril. The real conflicts were between Wayne and ex-wife Vera Miles who left her husband because of the obvious risks he was involved in, and their daughter (Katherine Ross) who was in love with Wayne's right-hand man (Jim Hutton), and is facing the identical situation. All the players took a back seat to the well-staged fire sequences photographed by William Clothier in Technicolor.

The actor kept his American-fighting-man image intact by appearing in several war films during the decade as well. He played two cameo roles in *The Longest Day*

(1962), and *Cast a Giant Shadow* (1966). In the former a massive, star-heavy cast was enlisted to re-create the D-Day invasion of Europe; Wayne played American Lt. Col. Benjamin Vandervoot. In the latter he was promoted to play General Randolph in the true story of Col. "Mickey" Marcus (Kirk Douglas) who helped fashion the Israeli army into a strong fighting unit in their struggle against the Arabs.

In Otto Preminger's large-scale production of *In Harm's Way* (1965), Wayne was a naval officer called upon for assistance after the deadly Japanese attack on Pearl Harbor wiped out most of our ships. Onboard Wayne's ship is Kirk Douglas as a moody executive officer who gives everyone a hard time. Wayne is ordered to engage the enemy in a hopelessly one-sided attack, forcing his battered ships to return to the harbor and putting him in the hospital with injuries. In the hospital he meets nurse Patricia Neal and falls in love with her. The

THE LONGEST DAY (1962). As Lt. Col. Benjamin Vandervoot

IN HARM'S WAY (1965). With Patricia Neal

film was entangled with too many threads of plot, including politics, young love, and a father-son conflict—and a large cast of seasoned players (Burgess Meredith, Dana Andrews, Franchot Tone, and others) coped vainly with trying to unravel them. Even the action sequences were poorly done with too many obvious miniatures utilized to simulate havoc. The film was directed by Preminger for Paramount Pictures release and continued his long string of lesser work turned out over the last two decades.

Wayne's most controversial production of the entire decade was his 1968 war story, *The Green Berets*.

Wayne's hawkish views on the Vietnam war were well known to everyone. He saw the battle as a noble effort on the part of the American people to protect the rights of a small nation which was being attacked by outside, Communist-inspired forces. As America's foremost spokesman of right-wing attitudes, he was not only appalled but disgusted at the spectacle of young Americans waving Viet Cong flags at rallies. It so irritated him that once again he wanted to make and direct a film which would be a combination of fictionalized history and pure entertainment. The result made those who supported his views quite happy and those who opposed literally livid with anger. When the film was released, there were pickets lined up outside many of the theatres. Congressmen, mostly confirmed "doves" regarding the war, made waves in the Senate, claiming that Wayne had used American men and property to express a slanted viewpoint of the way things really were overseas.

The screenplay for the film was written by James Lee Barrett and based on the best-selling novel by Robin Moore. Wayne co-directed with veteran special effects man Ray Kellogg. In the story, Wayne was a dedicated career officer who trains a group of men stationed at the John F. Kennedy School for Special Warfare at Fort Bragg, North Carolina. This crack special team of men had acquired the name of the "Green Berets" because of the headwear they sported. When the men are battle-ready, Wayne and the men go to Vietnam, where they are well used in repeated engagements with the enemy. Helping Wayne were Aldo Ray, Raymond St. Jacques, Jim Hutton and David Janssen (playing a war correspondant who changes his point of view), among a cast of thousands that mingled extras with actual fighting men. A vitally strategic town is taken and a special mission to capture a Communist leader is safely carried out.

The Green Berets took Wayne three grueling months to make on locations in Georgia and back on Hollywood sound stages. He had Green Beret members giving him technical advice.

When the film was finally released, it turned out to be a very good action film. Unfortunately many reviewers disagreed with Wayne's political viewpoint and instead of analyzing the film they spent most of their time criticizing the man. The movie, a Batjac Production released by Warners-Seven Arts, made a healthy profit. The excellent photography was done by Winton C. Hoch, the man who had won Academy Awards for *She Wore a Yellow Ribbon* and *The Quiet Man*, and the musical score was done by Miklos Rozsa, one of the real masters of the craft, noted for his scores of such films as *Ben Hur*, *Spellbound*, *King of Kings*, and *El Cid*.

The sixties had shown that Wayne had developed into an accomplished performer. For too many years people had been saying that he played only himself on screen, but any actor will tell you this is sheer folly to believe. The motion picture camera is one of the most revealing devices ever invented. With its ability to project a giant image for minute scrutiny, any degree of casualness or pretense can be sensed immediately by an audi-

THE GREEN BERETS (1968). As Col. Mike Kirby

ence. Wayne had the charisma and the ability to project an image more sincere than virtually any actor on the screen, past or present. Though hardly an actor with the stature of a Spencer Tracy or Paul Muni, he was, in his own work, the master of a complex craft.

As a person Wayne seemed to mature even more. His bout with cancer appeared to cause him to appreciate his work and the pure joy of living. The old joke that death is nature's way of telling you to slow down seemed somehow more relevant to him now that the end of the trail began to look a little closer. The ultimate destiny of man was becoming a fact he had to live with constantly as he watched many of his good friends succumb one by one: Grant Withers, Victor McLaglen, Ward Bond, James Edward Grant, Bruce Cabot and, perhaps most deeply felt of all, John Ford. This was not the time, he believed, to sulk and mourn but to take every day and do something with it that is important and vital. So the Duke goes on, working and enjoying himself and trying to please a public which continues to admire him.

Wayne's virtuoso performance in *True Grit* had climaxed another phase in the star's lengthy screen odyssey. His films of the sixties were rather simplistic extensions of his earlier work. Aided by wide-screen photography, colorful exterior locations in America and Mexico, and a determination to provide excitement without appealing to an audience's baser instincts, Wayne's Westerns offered a welcome counterbalance to the more violence-filled efforts being turned out for the younger viewers oriented to a permissive society.

But times change and Wayne, now over sixty years old, knew he would have to once again give the people what they wanted. Apparently they wanted blood—lots of it. The blood-and-gore syndrome that began in the late fifties when Hammer Films began to fill their horror remakes with stomach-churning scenes reached its zenith in the slow-motion glorification of violence in *The Wild Bunch* and *Bonnie and Clyde*. Wayne, reluctantly, gave in to the trend and some of his most recent work contains not only his, but the screen's most graphic bloodletting to date. (*Big Jake* [1971] had two of the bloodiest gunfights this writer has witnessed in films.) In a sense the violence could be considered a legitimate extension of reality long missing in the adult Western. We

THE SEVENTIES: THE TREND TOWARD REALITY

were so used to seeing our heroes being shot bloodlessly that it was a shock to see too much blood all at once. Thus the fun and games in the old West were passé and we saw in *The Cowboys* (1972) that our hero, Wayne, was not only shot and killed but was sadistically and literally blown apart by villain Bruce Dern.

Wayne's latest films also reveal other changes in his screen image brought about by his advancing years. Now most of the lovemaking is left to supporting players, with Wayne assuming the posture of a patriarch. As a substitute for female companionship he thrives on convivial banter with old regulars like Ben Johnson in *Chisum* (1970), preferring laughs to kisses. He even uses his age as a tool when, for example, his wife informs him in *The Cowboys* that the only help he can get to round up his cattle are all over sixty, and Wayne smilingly replies, "So am I." Now, more than at any other time, his own physical features convey the image we have of the real Westerner: furrowed, leathery, sun-spotted skin and gnarled hands. He has become a man as rugged in appearance as the land he rides on.

BIG JAKE (1971). In the title role

There were even greater changes in the man off-screen. For years Wayne had avoided television, preferring to work within the broader scope of movie screens. He would do an occasional role for John Ford and perhaps appear with Lucille Ball, but that was all. Now, after winning his Academy Award, you could find him all over the tube, appearing on comedy and talk shows. He made several appearances on *Laugh-In* and once came out dressed as a blue bunny-rabbit! Wayne would never have lowered himself for this nonsense in earlier years, but the time was now right to prove that he could be just as human as anyone else. Wayne even had his own ninety-minute special program in late 1970 that told the story of America by means of sketches and songs. The show was one of the highest rated of the year, and its repeat showing earned equally high figures.

In 1973 Wayne even went so far as to record an album of poetry. Called *America, Why I Love Her*, it was one of RCA's big sellers of the year.

The formerly remote superstar also began to meet more with the press. Interviews were constantly appearing and more often than not centered on his politics rather than his screen work. As always, Wayne's remarks were liberally spiced with positive views of America, even when many of the questions directed at him were patently loaded. As recently as January 1974, he was still taking on all challenges when men from the *Harvard Lampoon* asked him to debate them by goading him with an invitation couched in rudeness and sarcasm. "We've heard you're supposed to be some kind of a legend," they wrote. "Everybody talks about your he-man prowess, your pistol-packing, rifle-toting, frontier-taming, cattle-demeaning talents, your unsurpassed greatness in the guts department. But we at the *Harvard Lampoon* tend to doubt it." James M. Downey, the author of the challenge continued, "You think you're tough. You're not so tough. We dare you to have it out, head on, with the young whelps here who would call the supposedly unbeatable John Wayne the biggest fraud in history."

Wayne, well used to this kind of nonsense, replied: "Sorry to note in your challenge that there is a weakness in your breeding, but there is a ray of hope in the fact that you are now conscious of it." The incident was basically a publicity gimmick, with Wayne taking a print of *McQ* along with him to screen. After the movie he answered such penetrating questions directed at him from the audience as "What's the latest comic book you've read?" and "Is that real hair in your toupee?" Courtesy was apparently not one of Harvard's virtues that day, but the good sportsmanship of Wayne overcame the deficiency.

In spite of all these extracurricular activities, as well as looking after his two ranches and other personal investments, Wayne's main efforts were still concentrated in his picture-making. With the country in a constant state of internal turmoil and desperately in need of simple entertainment, Wayne decided to stay with the format he knew best, and his first six films of the seventies were all Westerns.

Directed by Andrew V. McLaglen, *Chisum* (1970) was almost a throwback to the old-fashioned story of the thirties in which we tended to portray outlaws as heroic figures. In those days Jesse James, the Younger Brothers, the Sundance Kid and others were all treated as if their crimes were the fault of an unfeeling society, and they became almost legendary heroes with their exploits. In *Chisum* we were presented a humanistic portrait of Billy the Kid. Wayne, as Chisum, was the owner of a huge cattle spread in New Mexico. Out to grab off most of the remaining land in the area, as well as Wayne's, was Murphy (Forrest Tucker). Onto the scene rides Billy the Kid looking for work and Chisum takes him on. The Kid, (Geoffrey Deuel) makes friends with an Englishman named Tunstall (Patric Knowles), and when Murphy has Tunstall killed, the Kid goes on a murderous rampage.

Chisum, though he appreciates the Kid's feelings, orders him off the ranch, and Billy heads to town for a showdown. He becomes trapped in a store and Chisum and his men ride to the rescue. In a hand-to-hand slugfest, Chisum puts an end to Murphy's reign of terror. Some of the best scenes in the film were between Wayne and pal Ben Johnson, who played his mumbling ranch foreman. Slickly photographed in Technicolor by William Clothier, the film was popular with the public.

Wayne's second film of 1970 was a weak copy of his earlier *Rio Bravo*. In *Rio Lobo*, directed by Howard Hawks, Wayne was an ex-Civil War officer who had the job of freeing a Texas town from a rampaging reign of terror carried on by a bunch of carpetbaggers. Routinely handled,

CHISUM (1970). With Ben Johnson and Forrest Tucker

RIO LOBO (1970). As Cord McNally

the film had only a few exciting moments, centered around a beautifully staged train-wreck sequence, and the wildly funny performance of Jack Elam, often the sadistic villain but here playing an amiable cowpoke in a change-of-pace role. The film had some of the worst dialogue ever heard in a Wayne film, and his leading lady, Jennifer O'Neill, was so awful that audiences couldn't wait for her scenes to end. *Rio Lobo* gains only fleeting distinction as a rough burlesque, which it was intended to be, of Hawks' and Wayne's earlier exemplary teaming in *Rio Bravo*.

Big Jake was the second release of a Wayne picture through National General (*Rio Lobo*, the first), a new company that lasted only a few short years. The film was as gory a film as Wayne had yet appeared in. Richard Boone precipitates a mass slaughter on Wayne's property and Big Jake McCandles (Wayne) goes after him and his gang with determined vengeance in mind. The resulting showdown turns out to be an even more grisly orgy of carnage. The film was directed by George Sherman, who had not guided Wayne in a film since the "Three Mesquiteer" series at Republic in the late thirties. Although Maureen O'Hara had major billing in the

THE COWBOYS (1972).
With Bruce Dern

film, she had a very minor role as Big Jake's wife.

Wayne's only film released in 1972 was *The Cowboys*, and it turned out to be one of his more unusual vehicles. As Will Anderson, Wayne finds his men running off to find gold and leaving him shorthanded with a large herd of cattle to drive to market. In desperation he stops by the local school and enlists the aid of a group of young boys. After training them, they set off on their trek, picking up Roscoe Lee Browne (in an excellent performance) as their cook. As the rough cattle drive progresses, the boys become men and fulfill their obligation with courage. Along the way Wayne becomes embroiled with Bruce Dern, brutally beating him up in a fight. In revenge Dern earned the hatred of Wayne fans everywhere by blowing their hero apart with a six-gun, the first such instance in which this had ever been done to Wayne. The boys carry on without their leader and wipe out Dern and his men as well as getting the cattle to their destination. Produced and directed by Mark Rydell, the film was fashioned from a screenplay by Irving Ravetch, Harriet Frank, Jr. and William Dale Jennings, from an original novel by Jennings. Though the Warner Bros. production was good, as well as interesting and different, it was not the sort of film Wayne fans wanted to see. *The Cowboys* opened in New York at the Radio City Music Hall, but was quickly pulled out when it failed to generate business at the box office.

In *The Train Robbers* (1973) Wayne, Rod Taylor, Ann-Margret, Ben Johnson, Christopher George and Bobby Vinton were after a hidden cache of loot supposedly buried in the desert in the wreckage of an old train. The Wayne contingent was pursued across the sandscape by the ex-partners of Ann-Margret's husband, who had originally hidden the loot. The main enjoyment was in the humorous dialogue between Wayne, Taylor, Ben Johnson and Ann-Margret. Audiences particularly enjoyed Wayne's remark to Ann-Margret: "I've got a saddle that's older than you." Director Burt Kennedy managed to stage one sequence in which a gunfight in a small town resulted in the town's fiery destruction. (Kennedy seems to blow up or burn down buildings in every Western he directs.) *The Train Robbers* also had a "twist" ending and an ambiguous portrayal by Ricardo Montalban, but the movie added up to nothing more than a minor divertissement.

Wayne, it has been rumored, originally wanted to do *Cahill* (1973) as a straight cops-and-robbers film, but the story was so easily adaptable, and he liked to work out West

so much more, that it became typical Western fodder. The screenplay by Julian Fink and Rita M. Fink based on a story by Barney Slalter, had Wayne playing a tough law officer who was particularly unfeeling towards his two sons. The boys help an outlaw gang pull a clever robbery by letting them out of jail to commit the crime and then locking them up again afterwards to give them a perfect alibi. The boys later regret their move and try to make amends, but the gang will not let them go. After a complicated series of brawls, gunfights and general mayhem, the boys and Wayne appropriately do their duty. Andrew V.

McLaglen directed with casual skill, but one could only wonder when the director and Wayne would really create a film with a little more style and class. After all, it had already been ten years since *McLintock!*

The cowboy finally got to play his cops-and-robbers drama in civilian garb in his first film release of 1974, *McQ*. The Batjac and Levy-Gardner Production, released through Warner Bros., had an interesting plot about narcotics dealers who plan to steal drugs from the police department. The raid comes off successfully but the crooks find out that the stuff is only sugar; some crooked cops within the force had

CAHILL (1973). In the title role

already stolen the drugs for themselves. Wayne, as a tough cop, becomes involved when some of his fellow officers are killed. When the department disapproves his roughhouse tactics, they relieve him of duty, but he leaves the force and goes out hunting on his own, finally cracking the case.

There were some excellent auto chase sequences but by far too much bloodletting. (There are four bodies on display before the film is five minutes old.) Wayne handles himself well in the action sequences but the more somber and touching moments show him visibly uncomfortable. The dialogue is replete with "hip" phrases and characteristically "tough" dialogue. (At one point Wayne says, "If you're not leveling with me I'm coming back and iron your face," to one of his informers.) Colleen Dewhurst is very good in some romantic byplay with Wayne ("You're a bear," she says. "I don't like bears," and Wayne winds up in bed with her.) Eddie Albert and Clu Gulager were excellent as two policemen, each suspected of being the mysterious rogue cop. *McQ* was directed by John Sturges and filmed in Seattle.

No one can forecast what the future holds for Wayne on the screen. Time moves inexorably on. His greatest film triumphs have always depended upon strong scripts and even stronger direction, and both are in relatively short supply. To Wayne, an actor for forty-seven years and a major star for more than thirty, his work is his life, and the enthusiastic response of his audiences is the adrenalin that keeps him functioning at full capacity. There is no question he will continue to give the people his unique blend of action and excitement right to the final fadeout. As Veda Ann Borg said to Wayne in *Big Jim McLain*, "76 inches! That's a lot of man!"

McQ (1974). In the title role

BIBLIOGRAPHY

Agee, James, *Agee on Film*, Boston: Beacon Press, 1958

Baxter, John, *Hollywood in the Thirties*, New York: A. S. Barnes, 1968

Bogdanovich, Peter, *John Ford*, Berkeley: The University of California Press, 1968

Dickens, Homer, *The Films of Marlene Dietrich*, New York: The Citadel Press, 1968

Everson, William K., *A Pictorial History of the Western Film*, New York: The Citadel Press, 1969

Halliwell, Leslie, *The Filmgoer's Companion*, 3rd. ed., New York: Hill and Wang, 1970

Madsen, Roy Paul, *The Impact of Film*, New York: The Macmillan Company, 1973

Michael, Paul, *The Academy Awards: A Pictorial History*, New York: The Bobbs-Merrill Company, Inc., 1964

The New York Times Film Reviews, 1913-1968, New York: The New York Times and Arno Press, 1970

Nolan, William F., *John Huston: King Rebel*, Los Angeles, Sherbourne Press, Inc., 1965

Parkinson, Michael, and Clyde Jeavons, *A Pictorial History of Westerns*, London: The Hamlyn Publishing Group, Ltd., 1972

Ricci, Mark, Boris and Steve Zmijewsky, *The Films of John Wayne*, New York: The Citadel Press, 1970

Schickel, Richard, *The Stars*, New York: The Dial Press, 1962

Sennett, Ted, *Warner Brothers Presents*, New Rochelle: Arlington House, 1971

Shipman, David, *The Great Movie Stars: The Golden Years*, New York: Crown Publishers, 1970

Sternberg, Josef von, *Fun in a Chinese Laundry*, New York: The Macmillan Company, 1965

Tomkies, Mike, *Duke: the Story of John Wayne*, New York: Avon Books, 1971

Wood, Robin, *Howard Hawks*, New York: Doubleday and Company, Inc., 1968

THE FILMS OF JOHN WAYNE

The director's name follows the release date. A (c) following the release date indicates that the film was in color. Sp indicates Screenplay and b/o indicates based/on. Sil. indicates silent film.

THE DROP KICK. WB. 1927. *Millard Webb.* Sp: Winifred Dunn, b/o novel *Glitter* by Katherine Brush. Sil. Cast: Richard Barthelmess, Barbara Kent, Dorothy Revier, Hedda Hopper.

MOTHER MACHREE. Fox. 1928. *John Ford.* Sp: Gertrude Orr, b/o story by Rida Johnson Young. Sil. Cast: Belle Bennett, Neil Hamilton, Victor McLaglen, Ted McNamara.

HANGMAN'S HOUSE. Fox. 1928. *John Ford.* Sp: Marion Orth, b/o story by Donn Byrne. Sil. Cast: Victor McLaglen, June Collyer, Hobart Bosworth, Larry Kent, Earle Foxe.

SALUTE. Fox. 1929. *John Ford* and *David Butler.* Sp: John Stone, b/o story by Tristram Tupper. Cast: George O'Brien, Helen Chandler, Stepin Fetchit, Frank Albertson, Rex Bell.

WORDS AND MUSIC. Fox. 1929. *James Tinling.* Sp: Frederick Hazlitt Brennan and Jack McEdward. Cast: Lois Moran, David Percy, Helen Twelvetrees, William Orlamond.

MEN WITHOUT WOMEN. Fox. 1930. *John Ford.* Sp: Dudley Nichols, b/o story by John Ford and James K. McGuinness. Cast: Kennth MacKenna, Frank Albertson, Paul Page.

ROUGH ROMANCE. Fox. 1930. *A.F. Erickson.* Sp: Elliott Lester, b/o story by Kenneth B. Clark. Cast: George O'Brien, Helen Chandler, Antonio Moreno, Noel Francis.

CHEER UP AND SMILE. Fox. 1930. *Sidney Lanfield.* Sp: Howard J. Green, b/o story by Richard Connell. Cast: Arthur Lake, Dixie Lee, Olga Baclanova, Whispering Jack Smith.

THE BIG TRAIL. Fox. 1930. *Raoul Walsh*. Sp: Jack Peabody, Marie Boyle and Florence Postal, b/o story by Hal G. Evarts. Cast: Marguerite Churchill, El Brendel, Tully Marshall, Tyrone Power, Sr., Ward Bond.

GIRLS DEMAND EXCITEMENT. Fox. 1931. *Seymour Felix*. Sp: Harlan Thompson. Cast: Virginia Cherrill, Marguerite Churchill, Helen Jerome Eddy, William Janney, Eddie Nugent.

THREE GIRLS LOST. Fox. 1931. *Sidney Lanfield*. Sp: Bradley King, b/o story by Robert D. Andrews. Cast: Loretta Young, Lew Cody, Joyce Compton, Joan Marsh, Paul Fix.

MEN ARE LIKE THAT (Originally titled ARIZONA). Columbia. 1931. *George B. Seitz*. Sp: Robert Riskin and Dorothy Howell, b/o story by Augustus Thomas. Cast: Laura LaPlante, June Clyde, Forrest Stanley.

RANGE FEUD. Columbia. 1931. *D. Ross Lederman*. Sp: Milton Krims. Cast: Buck Jones, Susan Fleming, Ed LeSaint, Harry Woods.

MAKER OF MEN. Columbia. 1931. *Edward Sedgwick*. Sp: Howard J. Green and Edward Sedgwick. Cast: Jack Holt, Richard Cromwell, Joan Marsh, Robert Allen, Walter Catlett.

HAUNTED GOLD. WB. 1932. *Mack V. Wright*. Sp: Adele Buffington. Cast: Sheila Terry, Harry Woods, Erville Alderson, Otto Hoffman.

SHADOW OF THE EAGLE. Mascot. 1932. *Ford Beebe*. Sp: Ford Beebe, Colbert Clark and Wyndham Gittens. Cast: Dorothy Gulliver, Edward Hearn, Richard Tucker, Lloyd Whitlock, Walter Miller. A twelve-chapter serial.

HURRICANE EXPRESS. Mascot. 1932. *Armand Schaefer* and *J.P. McGowan*. Sp: Colbert Clark, Barney Sarecky and Wyndham Gittens. Cast: Shirley Grey, Tully Marshall, Conway Tearle, J. Farrell MacDonald, Matthew Betz. A twelve-chapter serial.

TEXAS CYCLONE. Columbia. 1932. *D. Ross Lederman*. Sp: William Colt Mac-Donald. Cast: Tim McCoy, Shirley Grey, Wheeler Oakman, Wallace MacDonald, Harry Cording.

LADY AND GENT. Paramount. 1932. *Stephen Roberts*. Sp: Grover Jones and William Slavens McNutt. Cast: George Bancroft, Wynne Gibson, Charles Starrett, James Gleason.

TWO-FISTED LAW. Columbia. 1932. *D. Ross Lederman*. Sp: William Colt MacDonald. Cast: Tim McCoy, Alice Day, Wheeler Oakman, Tully Marshall, Wallace MacDonald, Walter Brennan.

RIDE HIM, COWBOY. WB. 1932. *Fred Allen.* Sp: Kenneth Perkins and Scott Mason. Cast: Ruth Hall, Henry B. Walthall, Harry Gribbon, Otis Harlan, Frank Hagney.

THE BIG STAMPEDE. WB. 1932. *Tenny Wright.* Sp: Marion Jackson and Kurt Kempler. Cast: Noah Beery, Mae Madison, Luis Alberni, Berton Churchill, Paul Hurst.

THE TELEGRAPH TRAIL. WB. 1933. *Tenny Wright.* Sp: Kurt Kempler. Cast: Marceline Day, Frank McHugh, Otis Harlan, Yakima Canutt.

CENTRAL AIRPORT. WB. 1933. *William A. Wellman.* Sp: Jack Moffitt, Rian James and James Seymour. Cast: Richard Barthelmess, Sally Eilers, Tom Brown, Glenda Farrell.

HIS PRIVATE SECRETARY. Showmen's Pictures. 1933. *Philip A. Whitman.* Sp: Lew Collins. Cast: Evalyn Knapp, Alec B. Francis, Natalie Kingston, Arthur Hoyt, Al St. John.

SOMEWHERE IN SONORA. WB. 1933. *Mack V. Wright.* Sp: Joe Roach, b/o story by Will Levington Comfort. Cast: Shirley Palmer, Henry B. Walthall, Paul Fix, Billy Franey, Ralph Lewis.

THE LIFE OF JIMMY DOLAN. WB. 1933. *Archie Mayo.* Sp: David Boehm, b/o play by Bertram Milhauser and Beulah Marie Dix. Cast: Douglas Fairbanks, Jr., Loretta Young, Aline MacMahon, Guy Kibbee.

THE THREE MUSKETEERS. Mascot. 1933. *Armand Schaefer* and *Colbert Clark.* Sp: Norman S. Hall, Colbert Clark, Wyndham Gittens and Barney Sarecky. Cast: Ruth Hall, Jack Mulhall, Raymond Hatton, Francis X. Bushman, Jr., Noah Beery, Jr. A twelve-chapter serial.

BABY FACE. WB. 1933. *Alfred E. Green.* Sp: Gene Markey and Kathryn Scola, b/o story by Mark Canfield. Cast: Barbara Stanwyck, George Brent, Donald Cook, Margaret Lindsay, Douglass Dumbrille.

THE MAN FROM MONTEREY. WB. 1933. *Mack V. Wright.* Sp: Leslie Mason. Cast: Ruth Hall, Nena Quartero, Luis Alberni, Francis Ford, Donald Reed, Lafe McKee.

RIDERS OF DESTINY. Monogram. 1933. *Robert N. Bradbury.* Sp: Robert N. Bradbury. Cast: Cecilia Parker, George "Gabby" Hayes, Forrest Taylor, Al St. John, Earl Dwire.

SAGEBRUSH TRAIL. Monogram. 1933. *Armand Schaefer.* Sp: Lindsley Parsons. Cast: Nancy Shubert, Lane Chandler, Yakima Canutt, Wally Wales, Art Mix, Robert Burns.

COLLEGE COACH WB. 1933. *William A. Wellman.* Sp: Niven Busch and Manuel Seff. Cast: Dick Powell, Ann Dvorak, Pat O'Brien, Arthur Bryan, Lyle Talbot, Hugh Herbert.

LUCKY TEXAN. Monogram. 1934. *Robert N. Bradbury.* Sp: Robert N. Bradbury. Cast: Barbara Sheldon, George "Gabby" Hayes, Lloyd Whitlock, Yakima Canutt, Earl Dwire.

✓ WEST OF THE DIVIDE. Monogram. 1934. *Robert N. Bradbury.* Sp: Robert N. Bradbury. Cast: Virginia Brown Faire, Lloyd Whitlock, Yakima Canutt, George "Gabby" Hayes, Earl Dwire.

BLUE STEEL. Monogram. 1934. *Robert N. Bradbury.* Sp: Robert N. Bradbury. Cast: Eleanor Hunt, George "Gabby" Hayes, Ed Peil, Yakima Canutt, George Cleveland.

THE MAN FROM UTAH. Monogram. 1934. *Robert N. Bradbury.* Sp: Lindsley Parsons. Cast: Polly Ann Young, George "Gabby" Hayes, Ed Peil, Yakima Canutt, George Cleveland.

RANDY RIDES ALONE. Monogram. 1934. *Harry Fraser.* Sp: Lindsley Parsons. Cast: Alberta Vaughn, George "Gabby" Hayes, Earl Dwire, Yakima Canutt, Tex Phelps.

THE STAR PACKER. Monogram. 1934. *Robert N. Bradbury.* Sp: Robert N. Bradbury. Cast: Verna Hillie, George "Gabby" Hayes, Yakima Canutt, Earl Dwire, George Cleveland.

✓ THE TRAIL BEYOND: Monogram. 1934. *Robert N. Bradbury.* Sp: Lindsley Parsons, b/o story by James Oliver Curwood. Cast: Verna Hillie, Noah Beery, Noah Beery, Jr.

'NEATH ARIZONA SKIES. Monogram. 1934. *Harry Fraser.* Sp: B.R. Tuttle. Cast: Sheila Terry, Jay Wilsey, Yakima Canutt, Jack Rockwell, George "Gabby" Hayes.

LAWLESS FRONTIER. Monogram. 1935. *Robert N. Bradbury.* Sp: Robert N. Bradbury. Cast: Sheila Terry, George "Gabby" Hayes, Earl Dwire, Yakima Canutt, Jack Rockwell.

TEXAS TERROR. Monogram. 1935. *Robert N. Bradbury.* Sp: Robert N. Bradbury. Cast: Lucile Browne, LeRoy Mason, George "Gabby" Hayes, Buffalo Bill, Jr., Bert Dillard.

RAINBOW VALLEY. Monogram. 1935. *Robert N. Bradbury.* Sp: Lindsley Parsons. Cast: Lucile Browne, LeRoy Mason, George "Gabby" Hayes, Buffalo Bill, Jr., Bert Dillard.

PARADISE CANYON. Monogram. 1935. *Carl Pierson*. Sp: Lindsley Parsons. Cast: Marion Burns, Yakima Canutt, Reed Howes, Perry Murdock.

THE DAWN RIDER. Monogram. 1935. *Robert N. Bradbury*. Sp: Robert N. Bradbury. Cast: Marion Burns, Yakima Canutt, Reed Howes, Denny Meadows.

✓ WESTWARD HO. Republic. 1935. *Robert N. Bradbury*. Sp: Lindsley Parsons. Cast: Sheila Mannors, Frank McGlynn, Jr., Jack Curtis, Yakima Canutt, Dickie Jones, Hank Bell.

DESERT TRAIL. Monogram. 1935. *Collin Lewis*. Sp: Lindsley Parsons. Cast: Mary Kornman, Paul Fix, Edward Chandler, Lafe McKee, Henry Hull, Al Ferguson.

NEW FRONTIER. Republic. 1935. *Carl Pierson*. Sp: Robert Emmett. Cast: Muriel Evans, Mary McLaren, Murdock MacQuarrie, Warner Richmond, Sam Flint, Al Bridge.

LAWLESS RANGE. Republic. 1935. *Robert N. Bradbury*. Sp: Lindsley Parsons. Cast: Sheila Mannors, Earl Dwire, Frank McGlynn, Jr., Jack Curtis, Yakima Canutt, Wally Howe.

THE LAWLESS NINETIES. Republic. 1936. *Joseph Kane*. Sp: Joseph Poland. Cast: Ann Rutherford, Lane Chandler, Harry Woods, Snowflake, George "Gabby" Hayes, Charles King.

KING OF THE PECOS. Republic. 1936. *Joseph Kane*. Sp: Bernard McConville, Darrell McGowan and Stuart McGowan. Cast: Muriel Evans, Cy Kendall, Jack Clifford, Yakima Canutt.

THE OREGON TRAIL. Republic. 1936. *Scott Pembroke*. Sp: Lindsley Parsons and Robert Emmett. Cast: Ann Rutherford, Yakima Canutt, Frank Rice, Joe Girard, Harry Harvey.

WINDS OF THE WASTELAND. Republic. 1936. *Mack V. Wright*. Sp: Joseph Poland. Cast: Phyllis Fraser, Yakima Canutt, Lane Chandler, Sam Flint, Bob Kortman, Lew Kelly.

THE SEA SPOILERS. Universal. 1936. *Frank Strayer*. Sp: George Waggner, b/o story by Dorrell and Stuart McGowan. Cast: Nan Grey, Fuzzy Knight, William Bakewell, Russell Hicks.

✓ THE LONELY TRAIL. Republic. 1936. *Joseph Kane*. Sp: Bernard McConville. Cast: Ann Rutherford, Cy Kendall, Snowflake, Bob Kortman, Sam Flint, Yakima Canutt, Bob Burns.

CONFLICT. Universal. 1936. *David Howard*. Sp: Charles A. Logue and Walter Weems, b/o novel *The Abysmal Brute* by Jack London. Cast: Jean Rogers, Tommy Bupp, Ward Bond, Harry Woods.

CALIFORNIA STRAIGHT AHEAD. Universal. 1937. *Arthur Lubin*. Sp: Herman Boxer. Cast: Louise Latimer, Robert McWade, Tully Marshall, Theodore Von Eltz, LeRoy Mason.

I COVER THE WAR. Universal. 1937. *Arthur Lubin*. Sp: George Waggner. Cast: Gwen Gaze, Don Barclay, James Bush, Pat Somerset, Charles Brokaw, Earl Hodgins, Jack Mack.

IDOL OF THE CROWDS. Universal. 1937. *Arthur Lubin*. Sp: George Waggner and Harold Buckley, b/o story by George Waggner. Cast: Sheila Bromley, Billy Burrud, Russell Gordon.

ADVENTURE'S END. Universal. 1937. *Arthur Lubin*. Sp: Ben Ames Williams. Cast: Diana Gibson, Moroni Olsen, Montagu Love, Ben Carter, George Cleveland, Glenn Strange.

BORN TO THE WEST (also released as HELL TOWN). Paramount. 1937. *Charles Barton*. Sp: Stuart Anthony and Robert Yost, b/o novel by Zane Grey. Cast: Marsha Hunt, John Mack Brown, Monte Blue, James Craig, Lucien Littlefield.

PALS OF THE SADDLE. Republic. 1938. *George Sherman*. Sp: Stanley Roberts and Betty Burbridge. Cast: Ray Corrigan, Max Terhune, Doreen McKay, Jack Kirk, Ted Adams, Frank Milan.

OVERLAND STAGE RAIDERS. Republic. 1938. *George Sherman*. Sp: Luci Ward. Cast: Ray Corrigan, Max Terhune, Louise Brooks, Fern Emmett, Frank LaRue, Gordon Hart.

SANTA FE STAMPEDE. Republic. 1938. *George Sherman*. Sp: Luci Ward and Betty Burbridge, b/o story by Luci Ward. Cast: June Martel, Ray Corrigan, Max Terhune, William Farnum.

RED RIVER RANGE. Republic. 1938. *George Sherman*. Sp: Stanley Roberts, Betty Burbridge and Luci Ward, b/o story by Luci Ward. Cast: Ray Corrigan, Max Terhune, Polly Moran.

STAGECOACH. United Artists. 1939. *John Ford*. Sp: Dudley Nichols, b/o story *Stage to Lordsburg* by Ernest Haycox. Cast: Claire Trevor, Thomas Mitchell, John Carradine, Andy Devine, Louise Platt, George Bancroft, Donald Meek.

THE NIGHT RIDERS. Republic. 1939. *George Sherman.* Sp: Betty Burbridge and Stanley Roberts. Cast: Ray Corrigan, Max Terhune, Doreen McKay, Ruth Rogers, Tom Tyler, Kermit Maynard.

THREE TEXAS STEERS. Republic. 1939. *George Sherman.* Sp: Betty Burbridge and Stanley Roberts. Cast: Carole Landis, Ray Corrigan, Max Terhune, Ralph Graves, Roscoe Ates, David Sharpe.

WYOMING OUTLAW. Republic. 1939. *George Sherman.* Sp: Jack Natteford. Cast: Adele Pearce (Pamela Blake), Ray Corrigan, Raymond Hatton, Donald Barry, Yakima Canutt.

NEW FRONTIER. Republic. 1939. *George Sherman.* Sp: Betty Burbridge and Luci Ward. Cast: Ray Corrigan, Raymond Hatton, Phyllis Isley (Jennifer Jones), LeRoy Mason, Dave O'Brien.

ALLEGHENY UPRISING. RKO. 1939. *William Seiter.* Sp: P.J. Wolfson, b/o story *The First Rebel* by Neil Swanson. Cast: Claire Trevor, George Sanders, Brian Donlevy, Robert Barrat.

DARK COMMAND. Republic. 1940. *Raoul Walsh.* Sp: Grover Jones, Lionel Houser and F. Hugh Herbert, b/o novel by W.R. Burnett. Cast: Claire Trevor, Walter Pidgeon, Roy Rogers.

THREE FACES WEST (also released as THE REFUGEE). Republic. 1940. *Bernard Vorhaus.* Sp: F. Hugh Herbert, Joseph Moncure March and Samuel Ornitz. Cast: Sigrid Gurie, Charles Coburn, Wade Boteler, Trevor Bardette, Russell Simpson.

THE LONG VOYAGE HOME. United Artists. 1940. *John Ford.* Sp: Dudley Nichols, b/o the title and other one act plays by Eugene O'Neill. Cast: Thomas Mitchell, Ian Hunter, Barry Fitzgerald, Ward Bond, Mildred Natwick, John Qualen, Arthur Shields, Joseph Sawyer.

SEVEN SINNERS. Universal. 1940. *Tay Garnett.* Sp: John Meehan and Harry Tugend, b/o story by Ladislas Fodor and Laslo Vadnay. Cast: Marlene Dietrich, Broderick Crawford, Mischa Auer, Albert Dekker, Billy Gilbert, Anna Lee, Oscar Homolka, Samuel S. Hinds, Reginald Denny.

A MAN BETRAYED. Republic. 1941. *John H. Auer.* Sp: Isabel Dawn, b/o story by Jack Moffitt. Cast: Frances Dee, Edward Ellis, Wallace Ford, Ward Bond, Harold Huber, Tim Ryan.

LADY FROM LOUISIANA. Republic. 1941. *Bernard Vorhaus.* Sp: Vera Caspary, Michael Hogan and Guy Endore, b/o story by Edward James and Francis Faragoh. Cast: Ona Munson, Ray Middleton, Henry Stephenson, Helen Westley, Jack Pennick, Dorothy Dandridge.

THE SHEPHERD OF THE HILLS. Paramount. 1941. (c). *Henry Hathaway.* Sp: Grover Jones and Stuart Anthony, b/o novel by Harold Bell Wright. Cast: Betty Field, Harry Carey, Beulah Bondi, James Barton, Ward Bond, Marc Lawrence. Wayne's first color film.

LADY FOR A NIGHT. Republic. 1941. *Leigh Jason.* Sp: Isabel Dawn and Boyce DeGaw, b/o story by Garrett Fort. Cast: Joan Blondell, Ray Middleton, Philip Merivale, Blanche Yurka.

REAP THE WILD WIND. Paramount. 1942. (c). *Cecil B. DeMille.* Sp: Alan LeMay, Charles Bennett and Jesse Lasky, Jr., b/o story by Thelma Strabel. Cast: Ray Milland, Paulette Goddard, Raymond Massey, Robert Preston, Susan Hayward, Lynne Overman.

THE SPOILERS. Universal. 1942. *Ray Enright.* Sp: Lawrence Hazard and Tom Reed, b/o novel by Rex Beach. Cast: Marlene Dietrich, Randolph Scott, Margaret Lindsay, Harry Carey, Richard Barthelmess, William Farnum, George Cleveland. Samuel S. Hinds.

IN OLD CALIFORNIA. Republic. 1942. *William McGann.* Sp: Gertrude Purcell and Frances Hyland, b/o story by J. Robert Bren and Gladys Atwater. Cast: Binnie Barnes, Albert Dekker, Helen Parrish, Patsy Kelly, Edgar Kennedy, Dick Purcell.

FLYING TIGERS. Republic. 1942. *David Miller.* Sp: Kenneth Gamet and Barry Trivers, b/o story by Gamet. Cast: John Carroll, Anna Lee, Paul Kelly, Gordon Jones, Mae Clarke, Tom Neal.

REUNION IN FRANCE. MGM. 1942. *Jules Dassin.* Sp: Jan Lustig, b/o story by Ladislas Bus-Fekete. Cast: Joan Crawford, Philip Dorn, Reginald Owen, Albert Bassermann, John Carradine.

PITTSBURGH. Universal. 1942. *Lewis Seiler.* Sp: Kenneth Gamet and Tom Reed, b/o story by George Olsen and Tom Reed. Cast: Marlene Dietrich, Randolph Scott, Frank Craven, Louise Allbritton, Thomas Gomez, Ludwig Stossel, Shemp Howard, Douglas Fowley, Samuel S. Hinds.

A LADY TAKES A CHANCE. RKO. 1943. *William A. Seiter.* Sp: Robert Ardrey, b/o story by Jo Swerling. Cast: Jean Arthur, Charles Winninger, Phil Silvers, Don Costello, Grant Withers.

IN OLD OKLAHOMA (also released as WAR OF THE WILDCATS). Republic. 1943. *Albert S. Rogell*. Sp: Ethel Hill and Eleanore Griffin, b/o story by Thomson Burtis. Cast: Martha Scott, Albert Dekker, George "Gabby" Hayes, Dale Evans, Grant Withers, Marjorie Rambeau, Paul Fix.

THE FIGHTING SEABEES. Republic. 1944. *Howard Lydecker* and *Edward Ludwig*. Sp: Borden Chase and Aeneas MacKenzie, b/o story by Chase. Cast: Susan Hayward, Dennis O'Keefe, William Frawley, Addison Richards, Paul Fix, Grant Withers, Leonid Kinskey.

TALL IN THE SADDLE. RKO. 1944. *Edwin L. Marin*. Sp: Michael Hogan and Paul J. Fix, b/o story by Gordon Ray Young. Cast: Ella Raines, Ward Bond, George "Gabby" Hayes, Audrey Long.

FLAME OF THE BARBARY COAST. Republic. 1945. *Joseph Kane*. Sp: Bordon Chase. Cast: Ann Dvorak, Joseph Schildkraut, William Frawley, Virginia Grey, Russell Hicks, Paul Fix.

BACK TO BATAAN. RKO. 1945. *Edward Dmytryk*. Sp: Ben Barzman and Richard Landau, b/o story by Aeneas MacKenzie and William Gordon. Cast: Anthony Quinn, Beulah Bondi, Richard Loo.

DAKOTA. Republic. 1945. *Joseph Kane*. Sp: Lawrence Hazard and Howard Estabrook, b/o story by Carl Foreman. Cast: Vera Hruba Ralston, Walter Brennan, Ward Bond, Ona Munson.

THEY WERE EXPENDABLE. MGM. 1945. *John Ford*. Sp: Lt. Commander Frank Wead, b/o story by William L. White. Cast: Robert Montgomery, Donna Reed, Jack Holt, Ward Bond, Leon Ames.

WITHOUT RESERVATIONS. RKO. 1946. *Mervyn LeRoy*. Sp: Andrew Solt, b/o novel by Jane Allen and Mae Livingston. Cast: Claudette Colbert, Don DeFore, Anne Triola, Phil Brown.

ANGEL AND THE BADMAN. Republic. 1947. *James Edward Grant*. Sp: James Edward Grant. Cast: Gail Russell, Harry Carey, Bruce Cabot, Irene Rich, Lee Dixon, Tom Powers, Paul Hurst.

TYCOON. RKO. 1947. (c). *Richard Wallace*. Sp: Borden Chase and John Twist, b/o novel by C.E. Scoggins. Cast: Laraine Day, Sir Cedric Hardwicke, James Gleason, Anthony Quinn, Paul Fix.

FORT APACHE. RKO. 1948. *John Ford*. Sp: Frank S. Nugent, b/o story *Massacre* by James Warner Bellah. Cast: Henry Fonda, Shirley Temple, Pedro Armendariz, Ward Bond, Irene Rich, John Agar, George O'Brien, Anna Lee, Victor McLaglen, Dick Foran.

147

RED RIVER. United Artists. 1948. *Howard Hawks.* Sp: Borden Chase and Charles Schnee, b/o story *The Chisholm Trail* by Borden Chase. Cast: Montgomery Clift, Walter Brennan, Joanne Dru, Harry Carey, Sr., John Ireland, Coleen Gray, Harry Carey, Jr., Paul Fix.

✓ THREE GODFATHERS. MGM. 1948. (c). *John Ford.* Sp: Laurence Stallings and Frank S. Nugent, b/o story by Peter B. Kyne. Cast: Pedro Armendariz, Harry Carey, Jr., Ward Bond, Mae Marsh.

WAKE OF THE RED WITCH. Republic. 1948. *Edward Ludwig.* Sp: Harry Brown and Kenneth Gamet, b/o novel by Garland Roark. Cast: Gail Russell, Gig Young, Adele Mara, Luther Adler, Paul Fix.

✓ SHE WORE A YELLOW RIBBON. RKO. 1949. (c). *John Ford.* Sp: Frank S. Nugent and Laurence Stallings, b/o story by James Warner Bellah. Cast: Joanne Dru, John Agar, Ben Johnson, Harry Carey, Jr., Victor McLaglen, Mildred Natwick, George O'Brien, Tom Tyler.

THE FIGHTING KENTUCKIAN. Republic. 1949. *George Waggner.* Sp: George Waggner. Cast: Vera Ralston, Philip Dorn, Oliver Hardy, Marie Windsor, John Howard, Hugo Haas, Paul Fix.

SANDS OF IWO JIMA. Republic. 1949. *Allan Dwan.* Sp: Harry Brown and James Edward Grant, b/o story by Brown. Cast: John Agar, Adele Mara, Forrest Tucker, Wally Cassell, James Brown, Richard Webb, Arthur Franz, Julie Bishop. Wayne received his first Academy Award nomination for this film.

RIO GRANDE. Republic. 1950. *John Ford.* Sp: James Kevin McGuinness, b/o story *Mission With No Record* by James Warner Bellah. Cast: Maureen O'Hara, Ben Johnson, J. Carrol Naish, Victor McLaglen, Chill Wills, Harry Carey, Jr., Grant Withers, Sons of the Pioneers.

✓ OPERATION PACIFIC. WB. 1951. *George Waggner.* Sp: George Waggner. Cast: Patricia Neal, Ward Bond, Scott Forbes, Philip Carey, Martin Milner, Jack Pennick, Paul Picerni.

FLYING LEATHERNECKS. RKO. 1951. (c). *Nicholas Ray.* Sp: James Edward Grant, b/o story by Kenneth Gamet. Cast: Robert Ryan, Don Taylor, Janis Carter, Jay C. Flippen, James Bell.

THE QUIET MAN. Republic. 1952 (c). *John Ford*. Sp: Frank S. Nugent, b/o story by Maurice Walsh. Cast: Maureen O'Hara, Barry Fitzgerald, Ward Bond, Victor McLaglen, Mildred Natwick, Francis Ford, Eileen Crowe, Arthur Shields, Patrick Wayne, Michael Wayne, Melinda Wayne, Anthony Wayne.

BIG JIM McLAIN. WB. 1952. *Edward Ludwig*. Sp: James Edward Grant, Richard English and Eric Taylor, b/o story by English. Cast: Nancy Olson, James Arness, Alan Napier, Gayne Whitman.

TROUBLE ALONG THE WAY. WB. 1953. *Michael Curtiz*. Sp: Melville Shavelson and Jack Rose, b/o story by Douglas Morrow and Robert Hardy Andrews. Cast: Donna Reed, Charles Coburn, Tom Tully, Marie Windsor, Sherry Jackson, Tom Helmore, Dabbs Greer.

ISLAND IN THE SKY. WB. 1953. *William A. Wellman*. Sp: Ernest K. Gann, b/o his novel. Cast: Lloyd Nolan, Walter Abel, James Arness, Andy Devine, Allyn Joslyn, James Lydon, Harry Carey, Jr.

HONDO. WB. 1953. (c). *John Farrow*. Sp: James Edward Grant, b/o story by Louis L'Amour. Cast: Geraldine Page, Ward Bond, Michael Pate, Lee Aaker, James Arness, Leo Gordon, Paul Fix.

THE HIGH AND THE MIGHTY. WB. 1954. (c). *William A. Wellman*. Sp: Ernest K. Gann, b/o his novel. Cast: Claire Trevor, Laraine Day, Robert Stack, Jan Sterling, Phil Harris, Robert Newton.

THE SEA CHASE. WB. 1955. (c). *John Farrow*. Sp: James Warner Bellah and John Twist, b/o novel by Andrew Geer. Cast: Lana Turner, David Farrar, Lyle Bettger, Tab Hunter, James Arness.

BLOOD ALLEY. WB. 1955. (c). *William A. Wellman*. Sp: A.S. Fleischman, b/o his novel. Cast: Lauren Bacall, Paul Fix, Joy Kim, Barry Kroeger, Mike Mazurki, Anita Ekberg, George Chan.

THE CONQUEROR. RKO. 1956. (c). *Dick Powell*. Sp: Oscar Millard. Cast: Susan Hayward, Pedro Armendariz, Agnes Moorehead, Thomas Gomez, John Hoyt, William Conrad, Ted de Corsia.

THE SEARCHERS. WB. 1956. (c). *John Ford*. Sp: Frank S. Nugent, b/o novel by Alan LeMay. Cast: Jeffrey Hunter, Vera Miles, Natalie Wood, John Qualen, Olive Carey, Henry Brandon.

THE WINGS OF EAGLES. MGM. 1957. (c). *John Ford*. Sp: Frank Fenton and William Wister Haines, b/o life and writings of Commander Frank W. (Spig) Wead. Cast: Dan Dailey, Maureen O'Hara, Ward Bond, Ken Curtis, Edmund Lowe, Kenneth Tobey, Henry O'Neill, William Tracy, Bill Henry.

JET PILOT. RKO (Released by Universal-International). 1957. (c). *Josef von Sternberg*. Sp: Jules Furthman. Cast: Janet Leigh, Jay C. Flippen, Paul Fix, Richard Rober, Roland Winters, Hans Conreid, Denver Pyle. Film was made eight years earlier, but held back from release by producer Howard Hughes.

LEGEND OF THE LOST. United Artists. 1957. (c). *Henry Hathaway*. Sp: Robert Presnell, Jr. and Ben Hecht. Cast: Sophia Loren, Rossano Brazzi, Kurt Kasznar, Sonia Moser.

I MARRIED A WOMAN. RKO (Released by Universal-International). 1958. *Hal Kanter*. Sp: Goodman Ace. Cast: George Gobel, Diana Dors. Wayne played a cameo role, his scenes being filmed in color and inserted in the black and white film as a plot device.

THE BARBARIAN AND THE GEISHA. 20th Century-Fox. 1958. (c). *John Huston*. Sp: Charles Grayson, b/o story by Ellis St. Joseph. Cast: Eiko Ando, Sam Jaffe, So Yamamura.

RIO BRAVO. WB. 1959. (c). *Howard Hawks*. Sp: Jules Furthman and Leigh Brackett. Cast: Dean Martin, Ricky Nelson, Angie Dickinson, Walter Brennan, Ward Bond, John Russell, Bob Steele.

THE HORSE SOLDIERS. United Artists. 1959. (c). *John Ford*. Sp: John Lee Mahin and Martin Rackin, b/o novel by Harold Sinclair. Cast: William Holden, Constance Towers, Hoot Gibson.

✓ THE ALAMO. United Artists. 1960. (c). *John Wayne*. Sp: James Edward Grant. Cast: Richard Widmark, Laurence Harvey, Richard Boone, Frankie Avalon, Patrick Wayne, Linda Cristal, Joan O'Brien, Chill Wills, Joseph Calleia, Ken Curtis, Veda Ann Borg, Aissa Wayne, Hank Worden.

NORTH TO ALASKA. 20th Century-Fox. 1960. (c). *Henry Hathaway*. Sp: John Lee Mahin, Martin Rackin and Claude Binyon, b/o play *Birthday Gift* by Laszlo Fodor, from an idea by John Kafka. Cast: Stewart Granger, Ernie Kovacs, Fabian, Capucine, Mickey Shaughnessy, Joseph Sawyer, Stanley Adams.

✓**THE COMANCHEROS.** 20th Century-Fox. 1961. (c). *Michael Curtiz*. Sp: James Edward Grant and Clair Huffaker, b/o novel by Paul I. Wellman. Cast: Stuart Whitman, Ina Balin, Nehemiah Persoff, Lee Marvin, Michael Ansara, Bruce Cabot, Bob Steele, George Lewis, Jack Elam.

THE MAN WHO SHOT LIBERTY VALANCE. Paramount. 1962. *John Ford*. Sp: James Warner Bellah and Willis Goldbeck. Cast: James Stewart, Vera Miles, Lee Marvin, Edmond O'Brien, Andy Devine, Woody Strode, John Qualen, Jeanette Nolan, Lee Van Cleef, Strother Martin, Ken Murray.

HATARI. Paramount. 1962. (c). *Howard Hawks*. Sp: Leigh Brackett, b/o story by Harry Kurnitz. Cast: Hardy Kruger, Elsa Martinelli, Red Buttons, Gerard Blain, Bruce Cabot, Eduard Franz.

THE LONGEST DAY. 20th Century-Fox. 1962. *Ken Annakin, Andrew Martin*, and *Bernhard Wicki*. Sp: Cornelius Ryan, Romain Gary, James Jones, David Pursall and Jack Seddon, b/o book by Ryan. Cast: Robert Mitchum, Henry Fonda, Robert Ryan, Rod Steiger, Robert Wagner, Richard Burton and many others. Wayne had cameo role as an American officer in this all-star epic.

HOW THE WEST WAS WON. MGM and Cinerama. 1962. (c). *Henry Hathaway, John Ford* and *George Marshall*. Sp: James R. Webb, Suggested by series *How the West Was Won* in *Life* Magazine. Cast: Carroll Baker, Lee J. Cobb, Henry Fonda, Karl Malden, Gregory Peck and many others. Another cameo for Wayne. He appeared in the Civil War sequence directed by Ford.

DONOVAN'S REEF. Paramount. 1963. (c). *John Ford*. Sp: Frank S. Nugent and James Edward Grant, b/o story by Edmund Beloin. Cast: Lee Marvin, Elizabeth Allen, Jack Warden, Cesar Romero, Dorothy Lamour.

McLINTOCK!. United Artists. 1963. (c). *Andrew V. McLaglen*. Sp: James Edward Grant. Cast: Maureen O'Hara, Patrick Wayne, Stefanie Powers, Yvonne De Carlo, Chill Wills, Jerry Van Dyke, Jack Kruschen, Bruce Cabot, Edgar Buchanan, Strother Martin.

CIRCUS WORLD. Paramount. 1964. (c). *Henry Hathaway*. Sp: Ben Hecht, Julian Halevy and James Edward Grant, b/o story by Philip Yordan and Nicholas Ray. Cast: Claudia Cardinale, Rita Hayworth, Lloyd Nolan, Richard Conte, John Smith, Henri Dantes.

THE GREATEST STORY EVER TOLD. United Artists. 1965. (c). *George Stevens.* Sp: James Lee Barrett and George Stevens. Cast: Max Von Sydow, Dorothy McGuire, Charlton Heston, Roddy McDowall and many others. Wayne, in a cameo, was the centurion who leads Jesus to the crucifixion.

IN HARM'S WAY. Paramount. 1965. *Otto Preminger.* Sp: Wendell Mayes, b/o novel by James Bassett. Cast: Kirk Douglas, Patricia Neal, Tom Tryon, Bruce Cabot, Brandon de Wilde, Dana Andrews.

THE SONS OF KATIE ELDER. Paramount. 1965. (c). *Henry Hathaway.* Sp: William H. Wright, Allan Weiss and Harry Essex, b/o story by Talbot Jennings. Cast: Dean Martin, Martha Hyer, Michael Anderson, Jr., Earl Holliman, Jeremy Slate, George Kennedy.

CAST A GIANT SHADOW. United Artists. 1966. (c). *Melville Shavelson.* Sp: Melville Shavelson, b/o biography by Ted Berkman. Cast: Kirk Douglas, Yul Brynner, Senta Berger, Angie Dickinson, Luther Adler. Another cameo, with Wayne playing an Army General this time.

THE WAR WAGON. Universal. 1967. (c). *Burt Kennedy.* Sp: Clair Huffaker, b/o his book. Cast: Kirk Douglas, Howard Keel, Robert Walker, Keenan Wynn, Bruce Cabot, Gene Evans, Valora Nolan.

EL DORADO. Paramount. 1967. (c). *Howard Hawks.* Sp: Leigh Brackett, b/o novel *The Stars in Their Courses* by Harry Brown. Cast: Robert Mitchum, James Caan, Charlene Holt, Arthur Hunnicutt, R.G. Armstrong, Edward Asner, Paul Fix.

THE GREEN BERETS. WB-Seven Arts. 1968. (c). *John Wayne* and *Ray Kellogg.* Sp: James Lee Barrett, b/o novel by Robin Moore. Cast: David Janssen, Jim Hutton, Aldo Ray, Raymond St. Jacques, Bruce Cabot, Jack Soo, Patrick Wayne, Mike Henry.

HELLFIGHTERS. Universal. 1968. (c). *Andrew V. McLaglen.* Sp: Claire Huffaker. Cast: Katherine Ross, Vera Miles, Jim Hutton, Jay C. Flippen, Bruce Cabot.

TRUE GRIT. Paramount. 1969. (c). *Henry Hathaway*. Sp: Marguerite Roberts, b/o novel by Charles Portis. Cast: Glen Campbell, Kim Darby, Jeremy Slate, Robert Duvall, Dennis Hopper, Alfred Ryder, Strother Martin. Wayne won his Academy Award as Best Actor for his role as "Rooster Cogburn."

THE UNDEFEATED. 20th Century-Fox. 1969. (c). *Andrew V. McLaglen*. Sp: James Lee Barrett, b/o story by Stanley L. Hough. Cast: Rock Hudson, Antonio Aguilar, Roman Gabriel.

CHISUM. WB. 1970. (c). *Andrew V. McLaglen*. Sp: Andrew J. Fenady. Cast: Forrest Tucker, Christopher George, Ben Johnson, Glenn Corbett, Andrew Prine, Bruce Cabot, Geoffrey Deuel.

RIO LOBO. National General. 1970. (c). *Howard Hawks*. Sp: Leigh Brackett, Burton Wohl, b/o story by Wohl. Cast: Jorge Rivero, Jennifer O'Neill, Jack Elam, George Plimpton, Victor French.

BIG JAKE. National General. 1971. (c). *George Sherman*. Sp: Harry Julian Fink and R.M. Fink. Cast: Richard Boone, Maureen O'Hara, Patrick Wayne, Chris Mitchum, Bobby Vinton, Bruce Cabot.

THE COWBOYS. WB. 1972. (c). *Mark Rydell*. Sp: Irving Ravetch, Harriet Frank, Jr., William Dale Jennings, b/o novel by Jennings. Cast: Roscoe Lee Browne, Bruce Dern, Colleen Dewhurst, Slim Pickens, Lonny Chapman.

THE TRAIN ROBBERS. WB. 1973. (c). *Burt Kennedy*. Sp: Burt Kennedy. Cast: Rod Taylor, Ann-Margret, Ben Johnson, Christopher George, Bobby Vinton, Ricardo Montalban.

CAHILL. WB. 1973. (c). *Andrew V. McLaglen*. Sp: Harry Julian Fink and Rita M. Fink, b/o story by Barney Slalter. Cast: Gary Grimes, Neville Brand, Marie Windsor, Clay O'Brien, Morgan Paull.

McQ. WB. 1974. (c). *John Sturges*. Sp: Lawrence Roman. Cast: Eddie Albert, David Huddleston, James Watkins, William Bryant, Diana Muldaur, Julie Adams, Colleen Dewhurst.

✓ Rooster Cogburn (1975)

✓ The Shootist (1976)

INDEX

155

ABOUT THE AUTHOR

Alan G. Barbour is the author of *Humphrey Bogart,* a Pyramid Illustrated History of the Movies. He is also the author of *Days of Thrills and Adventure, A Thousand and One Delights,* and *The Thrill of It All,* all reflecting his lifelong devotion to films. A resident of Kew Gardens, New York, Mr. Barbour is the editor and publisher of *Screen Facts* Magazine.

ABOUT THE EDITOR

Ted Sennett is the author of *Warner Brothers Presents,* a survey of the great Warner films of the Thirties and Forties, and of *Lunatics and Lovers,* on the years of the "screwball" movie comedy. He has also written about films for magazines and newspapers. He lives in New Jersey with his wife and three children.